BILL HYLTON'S FRAME & PANEL MAGIC

POPULAR WOODWORKING BOOKS
CINCINNATI, OHIO
www.popularwoodworking.com

Read This Important Safety Notice

To prevent accidents, keep safety in mind while you work. Use the safety guards installed on power equipment; they are for your protection. When working on power equipment, keep fingers away from saw blades, wear safety goggles to prevent injuries from flying wood chips and sawdust, wear hearing protection and consider installing a dust vacuum to reduce the amount of airborne sawdust in your woodshop. Don't wear loose clothing, such as neckties or shirts with loose sleeves, or jewelry, such as rings, necklaces or bracelets, when working on power equipment. Tie back long hair to prevent it from getting caught in your equipment. People who are sensitive to certain chemicals should check the chemical content of any product before using it. The authors and editors who compiled this book have tried to make the contents as accurate and correct as possible. Plans, illustrations, photographs and text have been carefully checked. All instructions, plans and projects should be carefully read, studied and understood before beginning construction. In some photos, power tool guards have been removed to more clearly show the operation being demonstrated. Always use all safety guards and attachments that come with your power tools. Due to the variability of local conditions, construction materials, skill levels, etc., neither the author nor Popular Woodworking Books assumes any responsibility for any accidents, injuries, damages or other losses incurred resulting from the material presented in this book. Prices listed for supplies and equipment were current at the time of publication and are subject to change. Glass shelving should have all edges polished and must be tempered. Untempered glass shelves may shatter and can cause serious bodily injury. Tempered shelves are very strong and if they break will just crumble, minimizing personal injury.

Metric Conversion Chart

TO CONVERT	TO	MULTIPLY BY
Inches	Centimeters	2.54
Centimeters	Inches	0.4
Feet	Centimeters	30.5
Centimeters	Feet	0.03
Yards	Meters	0.9
Meters	Yards	1.1

Distributed in Canada by Fraser Direct
100 Armstrong Avenue
Georgetown, Ontario L7G 5S4
Canada

Distributed in the U.K. and Europe by David & Charles
Brunel House
Newton Abbot
Devon TQ12 4PU
England
Tel: (+44) 1626 323200
Fax: (+44) 1626 323319
E-mail: mail@davidandcharles.co.uk

Distributed in Australia by Capricorn Link
P.O. Box 704
Windsor, NSW 2756
Australia

Visit our Web site at www.popularwoodworking.com for information on more resources for woodworkers.

Other fine Popular Woodworking Books are available from your local bookstore or direct from the publisher.

09 08 07 06 05   5 4 3 2 1

Library of Congress Cataloging-in-Publication Data

Hylton, William H.
   Bill Hylton's frame & panel magic / Bill Hylton.
      p.   cm.
   Includes index.
   ISBN 1-55870-740-9 (pbk: alk. paper)
   1. Woodwork. 2. Cabinetwork. I. Title: Bill Hylton's frame and panel magic. II. Title: Frame & panel magic. III. Title.
TT180.H88 2005
684.1'042--dc22   2005012736

ACQUISITIONS EDITOR: Jim Stack
EDITOR: Amy Hattersley
DESIGNER: Brian Roeth
TECHNICAL ILLUSTRATOR: Jim Stack
PRODUCTION COORDINATOR: Jennifer Wagner

about the author

Bill Hylton is a longtime woodworker and woodworking writer. He writes a column on power-tool joinery for *Popular Woodworking* magazine and is a frequent contributor to *The Woodworker's Journal*. He has written many woodworking books, including *Rodale's Illustrated Cabinetmaking, Router Magic, Country Pine, Woodworking With the Router* (with Fred Matlack), *Handcrafted Shelves & Cabinets* (with Amy Rowland), *Chests of Drawers* and *Bill Hylton's Power-Tool Joinery.*

acknowledgments

Here are some names, a few well-known to woodworkers, but others unfamiliar. Fred Matlack, Phil Gehret, Paul Anthony, Ken Burton, Tony O'Malley, Andy Rae, Lonnie Bird, Nick Engler. These are among the many who taught me an awful lot about woodworking in general and frame-and-panel construction in particular. They wrote something, told me something or showed me something. I'm grateful for the knowledge they shared or the assistance they gave me.

In terms of this book, I'm grateful for the help of Jim Stack and Amy Hattersley of F+W Publications and my photo advisor, Donna Chiarelli.

I'm most grateful, of course, to my wife, Judi, who really put up with consequences of my addled work habits.

Thanks to all.

contents

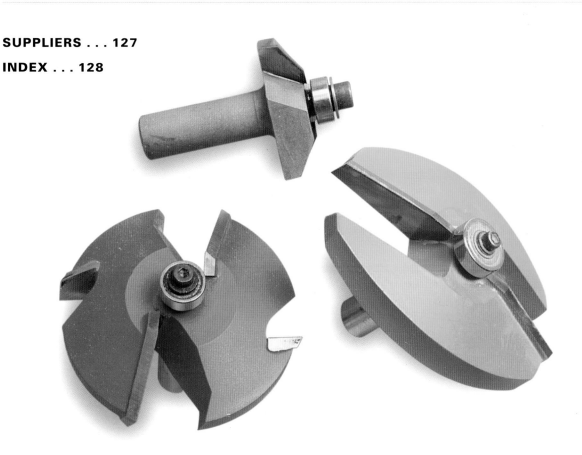

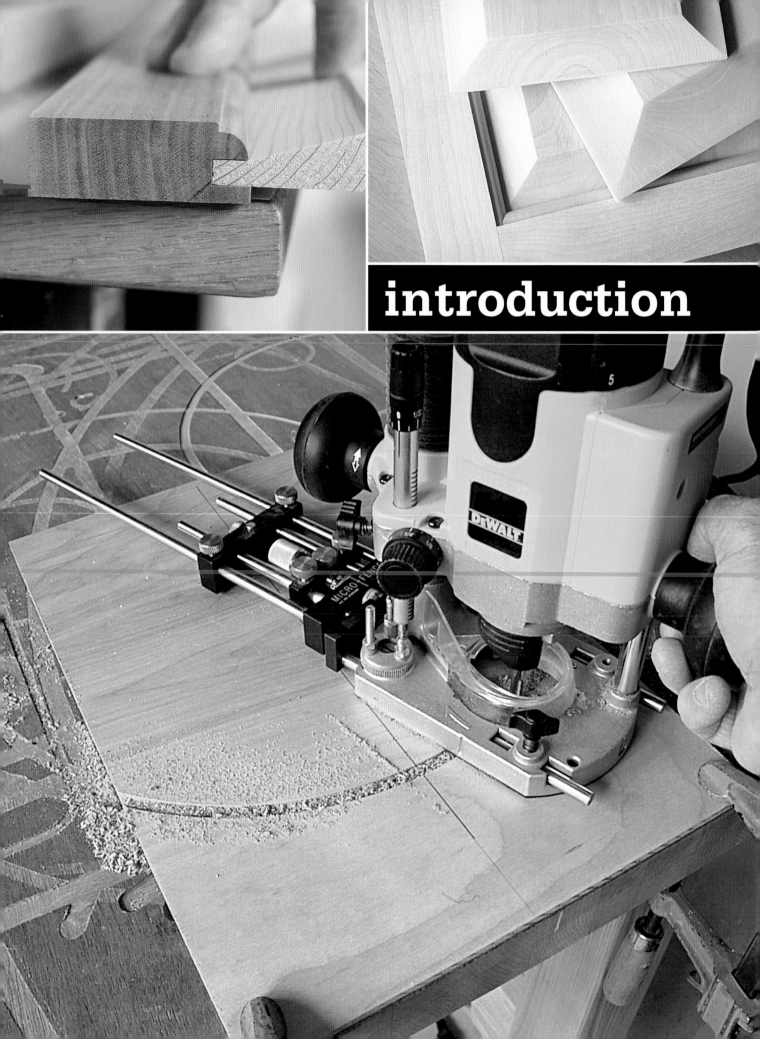

introduction

Framed panels draw the eye. We respond to the interplay of their wood surfaces just as we do to delicate dovetails or graceful cabriole legs.

Though they're something we most often think of in terms of cabinet doors, frame and panel assemblies can be used throughout casework — for case sides and backs, for example. In architecture, they're used for paneling as well as in door construction.

Frame and panel construction is rooted in the nature of wood. Wood moves, as we all know, and frame and panel construction is a way of dealing with that.

Wood scientists have contrived all sorts of stable materials from wood — plywood, oriented strand board, various particleboards. The rationale for frame and panel construction is largely moot.

But still we love the appearance.

So the modern, stable wood products are machined to look like frame and panel assemblies. Passage doors made of medium-density fiberboard (MDF) are milled to look like a traditional frame and panel construction, then painted to conceal their true composition.

If in considering frame and panel construction we think first of cabinet doors, it is because the doors (and drawer fronts) are the only parts of modern cabinetry that are made of real wood. The cabinets themselves are constructed of melamine or veneered MDF.

Most woodworkers think in terms of doors, of course, and that's a great place to start. But once you've tackled and mastered the craft of constructing doors for cabinets and cupboards, turn those tools and new skills to making the cabinets and cupboards themselves.

This book explores the full range of frame and panel construction, beginning with the equipment necessary. It explains traditional joinery as well as the quick, easy and beautiful router-cut cope-and-stick joinery. Raised panels, flat panels, veneered panels and curved-edge panels are covered. You'll read about glazed assemblies, too.

There is magic in frame and panel constructions. This book will help you capture that magic in your projects.

[CHAPTER *one*]

frame and panel fundamentals

The whole rationale for frame and panel construction stems from wood movement. If you go back a few centuries, furniture makers knew wood would expand in very humid conditions and shrink in very dry ones. They knew that this movement couldn't be constrained and that efforts to do so would cause splitting and buckling and broken joints.

Crotch-grained veneers on the multiple raised panels highlight this lidded chest I constructed for an article in *Woodworker's Journal* magazine. The frames for front, back and sides are joined with routed cope-and-stick joints. The gorgeous veneers were glued to walnut panels, and then raised.

PHOTO CREDIT:
Woodworker's Journal

Roughly patterned after chests built in Chester County, Pennsylvania, in the early 1800s, my tall chest has frame and panel side assemblies. The Chester Countians used mortise-and-tenon joints and mitered the sticking. I used cope-and-stick router bits.

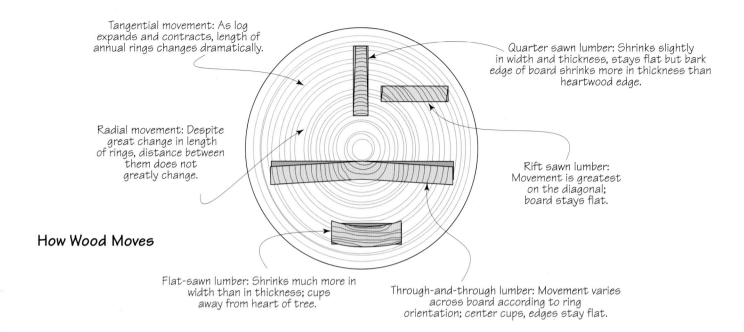

Tangential movement: As log expands and contracts, length of annual rings changes dramatically.

Quarter sawn lumber: Shrinks slightly in width and thickness, stays flat but bark edge of board shrinks more in thickness than heartwood edge.

Radial movement: Despite great change in length of rings, distance between them does not greatly change.

Rift sawn lumber: Movement is greatest on the diagonal; board stays flat.

How Wood Moves

Flat-sawn lumber: Shrinks much more in width than in thickness; cups away from heart of tree.

Through-and-through lumber: Movement varies across board according to ring orientation; center cups, edges stay flat.

An early solution was frame and panel construction. You know what I'm talking about. You have a frame made of skinny sticks, and the big opening is closed in with a big board. This is how it works: The frame is effectively stable, and the panel is mounted inside the frame in a way that allows it to come and go without causing any damage.

We all know that wood expands and contracts across the grain, but not as much along the grain. Expansion and contraction take place primarily tangentially to the growth rings in a log. There is change radially, of course, but the coefficient of that change is smaller than the coefficient of tangential change. In addition, different species of wood have different rates of change.

A newly sawn board doesn't always keep its shape as it dries. It can cup, bow, twist and diamond. Many of the changes can be predicted based on the way in which a board was sawn from the log.

Tangential vs. Radial Shrinkage

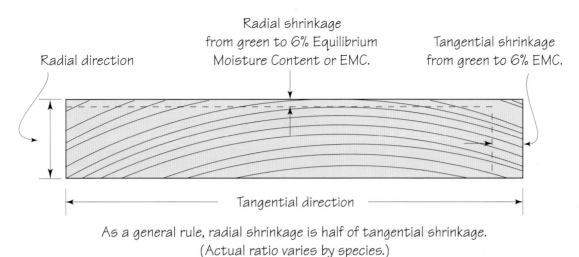

As a general rule, radial shrinkage is half of tangential shrinkage.
(Actual ratio varies by species.)

As wood expands and contracts with changes in temperature and humidity, the length of the cut growth rings changes dramatically, but the distance between adjacent rings changes very little. This explains the difference between tangential shrinkage (along the rings) and radial shrinkage (across the rings). It also explains why a flat-sawn board changes a great deal in width whereas a quarter-sawn board does not. Equilibrium Moisture Content and Moisture Content are two different values. Wood stored at a specific temperature and relative humidity will eventually reach EMC.

In practical terms: A flat-sawn board will change more than a quarter-sawn board, and this change from season to season isn't necessarily small. A red oak board expands and contracts more than a comparably dimensioned Honduras mahogany board.

The drawing at right shows a typical, albeit simple, frame and panel assembly. The arrows, which represent the expansion and contraction of the wood, are sized in proportion to the movement.

Note first that the height of the assembly is established by the length of the stiles, which are the vertical frame members. The grain runs vertically in them and in the panel. That dimension really isn't going to change, regardless of humidity levels, temperature or time of year. That's fixed.

The rails are the horizontal members captured between the stiles. The length of the rails won't change either.

Both the rails and stiles will expand and contract across their widths. Depending on the species and the actual width, these members will change by $\frac{1}{64}$" or $\frac{1}{32}$" or $\frac{3}{64}$" over the course of a

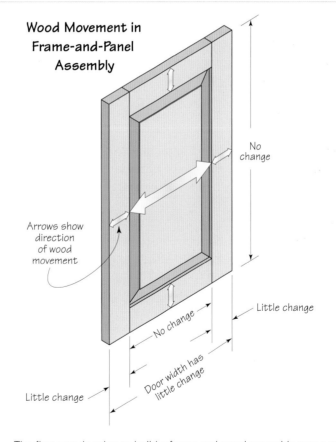

The first woodworker to build a frame and panel assembly was a magician, because he tamed wood's perpetual come and go. A broad panel, which changes considerably in width from season to season, is captured within a frame constructed of narrow sticks, which individually change very little in width. As you can see, the frame's dimensional change is negligible. It's a woodworking magic trick we take for granted.

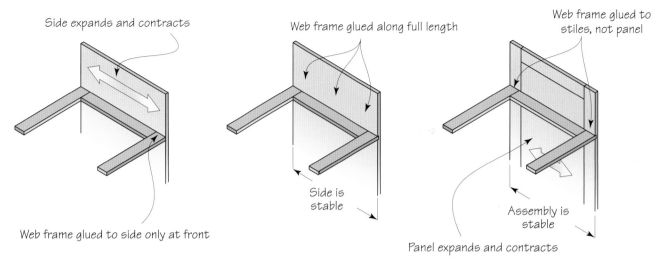

Solid-Wood Case   **Plywood Case**   **Frame-and-Panel Case**

year. So the frame is going to change in dimension by about $1/16"$, or maybe as much as $1/8"$.

The panel, because it may be four to six to eight times as wide as a stile, will expand and contract perhaps $3/16"$ to $1/4"$. But it is housed in a groove all around, and when properly fitted, it can change that much without bursting the frame. The panel moves a great deal, but the variation in frame dimension is still only about $1/16"$.

In practical casework terms, this assembly is a stable unit, like plywood. Look at the drawing above and compare the frame and panel case side with the solid-wood case side and the plywood case side.

If made of solid wood like red oak, a case side might expand as much as

$1/4"$ in width from winter to summer. If you glue a drawer runner to this side, across its grain, the glue joint is going to fail eventually. The panel will probably suffer as well. In summer, it may even buckle. Come winter, the panel will want to shrink, and because of the glued-in-place runner, it can't. Well, then it'll split, won't it?

But you can glue the runner to the two stiles — not the panel! — and have a sound construction. There's going to be a little bit of change out at the ends of the runner but not in the middle.

In terms of a door, you can fit this assembly into an opening with relatively little clearance. You have much less worry that it is going to swell and jam in the opening in summer.

JOINERY EVOLUTION

OK, so what's the payback? There's always a hitch, isn't there? Here it is: *work*. Making a frame and panel assembly is a lot more work than simply edge-gluing a pair or trio of boards to make a panel.

The furniture makers who, at least 300 years ago, originated frame and panel construction did it all with hand tools. You have to lay out and cut four mortises for a two-stile, two-rail frame. You have to plow the panel groove from mortise to mortise. You have to groove the rails from end to end. You have to cut tenons on the ends of the rails. You have to raise the panel. (They had those real wide boards 300 years ago, so instead of gluing up several narrow ones, they probably had to actually rip one down to the correct width!)

Now let's compound the work by adding a decorative profile around the inner perimeter of the frame, something to set off the panel. To incorporate this feature into the construction, you have to cut the profile along the frame pieces, from end to end. When you do the tenons on the rails, of course, this profile comes off. And when you assemble the frame, the profile looks goofy at the joints. You have to miter the joints and trim the profile from the stiles — more work.

Today, we don't usually chop out mortises, and we don't actually saw tenons by hand. But even with power tools — routers and hollow chisel mortisers and table saws — this is still a lot of work, expended simply to supplant one wide board.

Somewhere along the evolutionary line between 300 years ago and today, the shaper was invented. With it came the so-called cope-and-stick joint, a.k.a. the stile-and-rail joint or the rail-and-pattern joint.

It's an efficiency expert's dream system: One pass with each of two cutters replaces five separate and distinct operations.

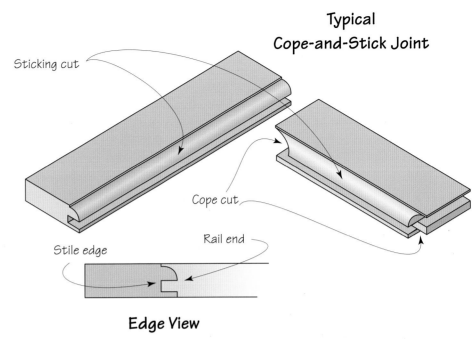

Typical Cope-and-Stick Joint

Sticking cut

Cope cut

Stile edge

Rail end

Edge View

Cope-and-stick joinery is attractive and adequately strong for most casework and lightweight cabinet doors. The joinery is formed with matching cutters. The sticking cutter plows a panel groove and a decorative edge profile simultaneously. The cope cutter shapes the ends of the rails to conform to the sticking.

The so-called sticking (or pattern or stile) cutter forms both the panel groove and the decorative profile in a single operation on one long edge of each rail and stile.

The cope cutter forms a stub tenon (or tongue) and the cope of the profile. The cope, which is the negative of the profile, fits snugly against the profile, and the stub tenon fits into the panel groove.

The trade-off — there's always a trade-off — is strength. The joint is easy to make, but it isn't nearly as strong as a mortise-and-tenon joint. Is it strong enough for the average frame and panel application? Apparently it is. I say "apparently" because this is one of those uncharted realms. People with a vested interest, like the bit manufacturers and industrial door makers, will argue that it is excellent, but reliable test information is hard to come by. I don't know of any reputable test of the strength and durability of the joint, though I'd bet some affected industry

has commissioned one.

Custom furniture makers often are dismissive of this construction. An example of this attitude is an online sneer I read about the joint being "OK for kitchen doors that aren't expected to last more than 10 or 15 years" but not satisfactory for an entertainment center's frame and panel side assemblies. I'm inclined to think that the typical kitchen cabinet door gets more of a workout than an entertainment center's side assembly.

I think the joint is fine for lightweight assemblies made from easily glued woods. For doors on cabinets and cupboards and for casework components made with common native hardwoods and softwoods, the joint is plenty strong, provided it is machined accurately and glued well. For heavier assemblies — architectural doors, for example — there are good ways to reinforce the cope-and-stick joint: dowels, screws, loose tenons. I'll mention these again in a little while.

PANELS

You may have noticed that I haven't said much about panels so far. That's because the panel is just along for the ride. Yes, it can contribute to the structural strength and integrity of an assembly, and it can also accelerate an assembly's demise. For the most part, the panel is a passive element, but let's fit it into the story.

Originally, a panel was raised on both sides with a plane. The practical reason for raising the panel is to reduce its thickness at the edge so it fits into the panel groove. When hand planing, the trick is to establish a taper that produces a match between the panel thickness and the groove width.

Today, a lot of woodworkers are content to raise panels on a table saw; they get the same tapered section that the old hand-planed versions had. Fitting the panel to the groove can be a little tricky, because the wedge shape of the edge is perfect for splitting out the groove walls. Misjudging the taper on the "safe" side can produce a panel that rattles in the groove.

Panels raised on the shaper or router table have a little tongue formed around the perimeter. If the panel is raised properly, the tongue just fits into the standard panel groove.

In addition, a shaped or routed panel can have a variety of bevel contours — coves with a bead, for example, and ogees, as well as the familiar flat bevel.

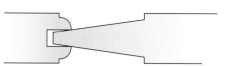

Traditional Planed Panel

Router-Raised Panel

Early woodworkers reduced the thickness of a panel by planing a bevel into both faces. The tapered section would fit into a narrow groove. Shrinkage across such a panel changes its fit to the groove, allowing it to rattle. In contrast, the fit of the router-raised panel is consistent from season to season, eliminating the rattle.

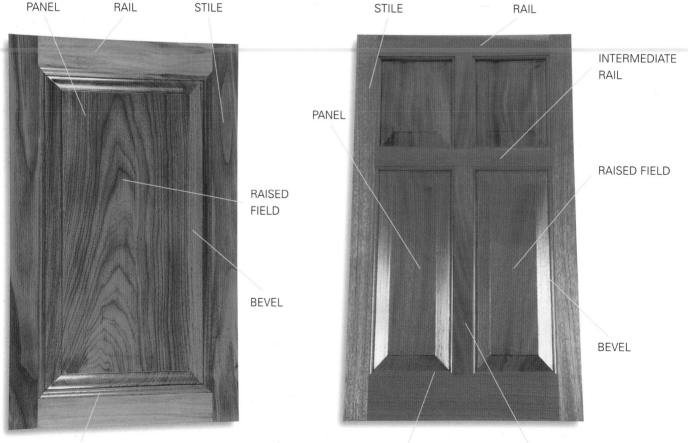

PANEL   RAIL   STILE

STILE   RAIL

INTERMEDIATE RAIL

PANEL

RAISED FIELD

RAISED FIELD

BEVEL

BEVEL

STICKING

STICKING   MULLION

TOOLS AND CUTTERS

The power tool that's showcased in cutting the joinery and raising the panels is the router. That's not to say it's the only tool that will do the work. If you have a mind to, you can make strong and attractive frame and panel assemblies without using the router at all, but using the router can certainly expedite the work. You can make very handsome, high-quality raised-panel assemblies with a modest ($1\frac{1}{2}$-horsepower) fixed-speed router and a benchtop router table.

I emphasize the modest horsepower because all too often the desire to make raised-panel doors fuels a lot of expensive purchases: high-horsepower router, multi-ring insert plate, height adjuster, microadjustable fence, tracks and accessories for securing holddowns and guides.

A big router and table setup is grand, and it's what I usually use. But don't let yourself be deterred from frame and panel work if all you have is smaller-scale equipment. Look at the bits you need to use, and from them establish just what sort of router you need.

The bits used to cut the frame profile and joinery generally are $1\frac{1}{2}$" to 2" in diameter. The smaller of these two bits — those $1\frac{1}{2}$ inchers — can be powered comfortably by a $1\frac{1}{2}$-hp router and safely spun at the router's 22,000-rpm speed. (See the drawing on this page.) The larger of these bits can be run at the same speed, but you might do better with 2 hp driving it.

The panel-raising bit is the fly in the ointment. Woodworkers immediately think of a $3\frac{1}{2}$"-diameter propeller as the baseline panel raiser. A bit this size shouldn't be run faster than 12,500 rpm, which makes a router with speed control essential. Moreover, to maintain that speed under cutting stress, you need more than $1\frac{1}{2}$ or 2 hp; you need 3 hp or even more.

You can find smaller bits in the horizontal orientation. These cut a scaled-down profile, of course, but because they are smaller, they can be run at higher speeds and with less power.

In addition, you can find vertical bits that cut full-scale profiles. Typically, the largest of these are $1\frac{1}{2}$" in diameter, and many are even smaller. As noted, a bit like this can be run at a router's cruising speed and needs only $1\frac{1}{2}$ hp to drive it.

As for the router table itself, know first off that you do need one for this work. The bits are not suitable for use in a handheld router.

Assess the size of table that's essential. In most cases — there are always exceptions — the frame members are slender, only 2" to 4" wide. You don't need a wide surface to support these workpieces. As for length, a couple of feet — 1' on either side of the bit — is sufficient to support the use of featherboards clamped to the fence, and you can work with even less infeed and outfeed support. Beyond that, expanses of tabletop are largely psychological in value.

The panel is the element that seems to call for more support. In truth, if you use featherboards to hold the panel against the table (when you are using a horizontal bit), you can cantilever most of the panel off the work surface. It does not need more support, though it may make you more comfortable to provide it. When using a

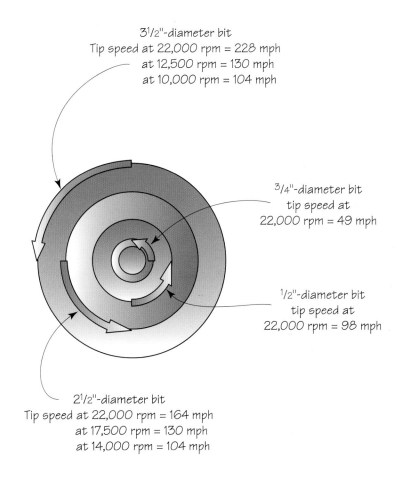

3$\frac{1}{2}$"-diameter bit
Tip speed at 22,000 rpm = 228 mph
at 12,500 rpm = 130 mph
at 10,000 rpm = 104 mph

3/4"-diameter bit
tip speed at
22,000 rpm = 49 mph

1/2"-diameter bit
tip speed at
22,000 rpm = 98 mph

2$\frac{1}{2}$"-diameter bit
Tip speed at 22,000 rpm = 164 mph
at 17,500 rpm = 130 mph
at 14,000 rpm = 104 mph

Tip speed illustrates the essence of router speed control. Each point along the cutting edge of a horizontal panel raiser travels a distance in a rotation of the bit. The further out from the center point you go, the faster the point must move to travel that distance. The critical point is the very tip of the bit. At 22,000 rpm, the tip of a $\frac{3}{4}$" bit moves at 49 mph, but the tip of a $3\frac{1}{2}$" bit moves at 228 mph. For optimum cutting performance with appropriate safety, limit tip speed to 130 mph.

vertical bit, the issue isn't the size of the tabletop but the height of the fence. Again, with a good trap fence or featherboard setup, you'll need far less fence surface than your intuition may goad you into providing.

Before spending a lot of money (really, *before* spending *any* money) on new equipment consider these options:

• A $1\frac{1}{2}$-hp fixed-speed router will satisfactorily drive typical cope-and-stick cutters as well as typical vertical panel raisers.

• A 2-hp router with speed control will handle those bits and midsize horizontal bits as well.

• A 3-hp router with speed control will handle any bits currently on the market, including those $3\frac{1}{2}$"-diameter horizontal raisers.

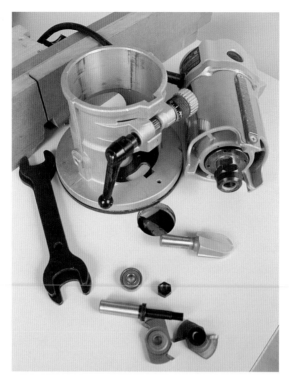

You don't need big bits and a powerful, variable-speed router for frame and panel work. A 1- to $1\frac{1}{2}$-hp router — a size that's pretty much extinct from the market — will drive smaller cope-and-stick bits, such as this reversible style, and vertical panel raisers. Mount the router in a table, either large or small, and you are ready to make doors and other assemblies.

A more powerful router has the moxie to spin the largest vertical panel raisers and most any cope-and-stick cutters. If equipped with variable speed, a 2-hp (at least) router will drive horizontal bits to $2\frac{3}{4}$" in diameter.

To efficiently spin the largest horizontal panel raisers, including those with backcutters, you need at least a 3-hp router with electronic variable speed. The speed controller not only enables you to reduce the rpms but helps the router to maintain the preset speed under loading.

Yes, you can raise panels on a benchtop router table. Here's my setup: a vertical bit powered by a $2\frac{1}{4}$-hp router, a tall fence with a trap auxiliary to guide the panel, and a featherboard, which is shimmed so it bears on the panel above the cut. The dimensions of the panel are irrelevant; so long as the panel edges are square and straight, you can raise the panel with this setup.

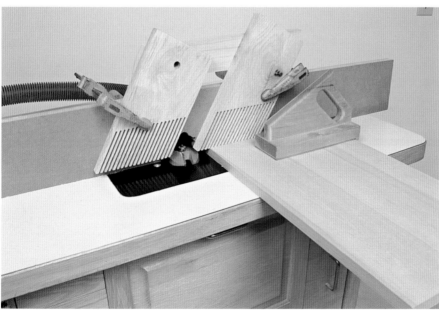

A big bit requires a bigger router, which generally means a bigger router table, but the setup isn't any more elaborate than the benchtop setup. The one-piece fence facing provides zero clearance around the cutter. The twin featherboards hold the work flat to the tabletop, and the homemade push block helps advance the panel across the bit.

[CHAPTER *two*]

making frames

Frame and panel construction begins with the frame. After you have the frame constructed, you can cut the panel to fit it. But always start with the frame.

The choice of appearance is the first decision, but the joinery is a close second.

The primary focus of this chapter is cope-and-stick joinery, which is cut quickly and easily with matched router bits. It's satisfactory for most cabinetry.

We'll also look at a variety of other joints that can be used, including mitered half-laps and the groove-and-stub tenon. First, though, I'll introduce you to the traditional approach — mortise-and-tenon joinery.

Many joinery options are available for constructing frames for panels. The primary choices — though certainly not the only ones — include (right to left) the traditional mortise and tenon, the mortise and tenon with mitered sticking, the fast and easy cope-and-stick and the cope-and-stick joint reinforced with loose tenons.

TRADITIONAL MORTISE-AND-TENON JOINERY

The quintessential frame joint is the mortise and tenon. It has proven through centuries of use to be strong and durable. It is the obvious choice if the frame needs to be extremely strong. Crafting the joint isn't inordinately difficult, but it does take time. A mortise-and-tenon frame will accept any sort of panel, from the traditional raised panel to a plain piece of plywood.

What such a frame doesn't have is any embellishment around its inner edge. To get that, you have a couple of options. One is to use separate molding (I'll discuss that beginning under "Applied Moldings" later in this chapter). Another is mitered sticking, which represents a new level of work.

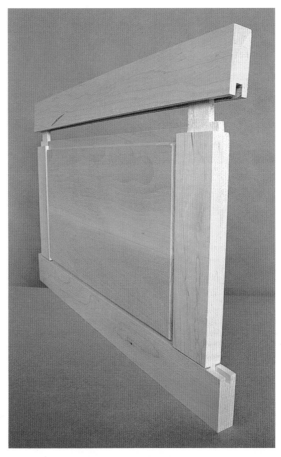

Traditionally, doors and other frame and panel assemblies are constructed with real mortise-and-tenon joints. This is a simple frame with square edges.

Lay out the ends of the mortises on both stiles at the same time. Use a square to scribe lines across the edges to delineate the edges of the rails, then the ends of the mortise. Account for the depth of the panel groove when you offset the mortise end from the rail edge. Allow about 1" of waste between the edge of the rail and the end of the stile — known as the "horn." (This is trimmed off after assembly.)

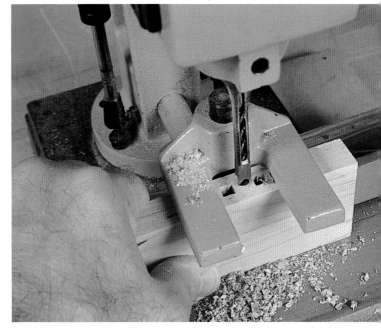

Excavate the mortises with a hollow chisel mortiser. Set up the machine to center the mortise across the stock; first make test cuts on scraps of the working stock. Cut the mortise ends first, then cut a series of separate holes between them. Finally, chisel out the webs between the separate holes.

A good way to form the tenons is with a dado stack set on the table saw. Clamp a standoff block to the rip fence, and use the miter gauge to feed the rail across the cutter. Butting the rail against the block positions it for the shoulder-forming cut. To remove any waste remaining between the shoulder and the rail end, slide the rail to the left and make a second pass over the cutter. Cut just the cheeks, not the edges.

Plow the panel grooves using the dado cutter set up with just the two outside blades. Set the rip fence to center the groove on the stock's edge. When you saw the groove, the inside edge of the tenon gets trimmed away.

Saw a haunch on the edge of the tenon that will be on the outside of the assembled frame. A haunch is a shoulder that fills the panel groove between the mortise and the end of the stile. Lay out the haunch, then cut away the waste with a band saw.

A dry fitting is in order after all the joints are cut. You should be sure the joints close tight and the assembled frame is square and flat.

SLIP JOINT

Years ago, before I mastered mortising, I used the slip joint instead of the mortise and tenon for simple door frames. I could cut both halves of a slip joint on my table saw using the same jig. The joint is very strong, but it doesn't look quite as clean as the mortise and tenon.

The slip joint, in case the name is new to you, is often called the "open mortise and tenon." There's good reason for this: The rails have a tenon, and the stiles have a mortise that's open at the top, bottom and one edge. Essentially, this open mortise is a notch.

A subset of the slip joint is the bridle joint, which joins the end of one piece to the middle of another.

A major advantage of the slip joint is the ease with which it is made. Its disadvantage emerges during assembly: In addition to clamping the tenon shoulder tightly against the mortise (as you do in all mortise-and-tenon glue-ups), you must clamp the mortise cheeks to ensure they bond to the tenon cheeks.

We were all beginners at some point. If you have a table saw, you can make a slip joint. If you have a table saw but no mortiser, no plunge router and no desire to test your hand-tool skills, even with an assist from a drill press, don't fret. Use the slip joint for your frame constructions.

For an inset door, face frame, web frame or other frame that will have its edges concealed, the slip joint is a strong, easy-to-cut option. Its only drawback is aesthetic: The edge and end of the tenon are visible on the edge of the assembled frame.

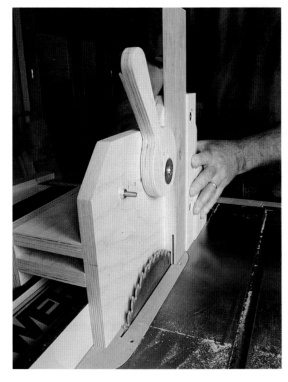

The slip joint notch in the stile can be sawed easily using any sort of tenoning jig. This one is my shop-made jig that straddles the rip fence. After cutting the tenons, adjust the jig's alignment so you can cut the notches. Because the panel groove will reduce the tenon width, you must adjust the notch depth by reducing the blade height.

A few extra clamps are needed to assemble a frame joined with slip joints. Pull the frame parts tight, shoulder to shoulder, with parallel jaw or bar clamps. Then apply a hand screw or C-clamp to pinch the cheeks of each joint tightly together.

MORTISE-AND-TENON WITH MITERED STICKING

Sticking is, of course, the profile cut on the edge of a frame's rails and stiles. If you stick the rails and stiles of a frame with mortise-and-tenon joinery, you need to trim the profile away from the shoulders of the joints and miter the ends of what remains to dress up its intersections. This step may seem a bit ticklish; it probably will be the first time you try it. Rest assured, it gets easier with practice.

Doors constructed this way are preferred by some furniture makers, because they are undeniably stronger than other types of joints and because it's appropriate for the sorts of furniture they make. In addition, the mitered sticking approach allows the use of a few profiles, such as the quirk-and-bead, that can't be cut by a cutter that addresses the edge of the workpiece (rather than the face).

In exchange for these benefits, you confront an assembly that's more time-consuming and demanding to make.

The work begins with careful layout of the mortise-and-tenon joints. Mark precise layout lines across an edge of each stile, delineating the edges of the rails, the width of the sticking, and the width of the mortise.

Crosscut the rails to length, accounting for both tenons and the sticking in your length calculation. (From the final door width, subtract the width of the two stiles, then add back the width of the sticking on each stile plus the length of the two tenons.)

Cut the mortises and the tenons. Fit the joints, and make sure the assembled frame is square and flat, with faces flush.

Next, rout the sticking and plow the panel groove. Usually, the panel groove is as deep as the sticking is wide. As long as it is no deeper than that, the groove can be plowed end to end because it will be trimmed off during the process of mitering the sticking. In ad-

This is the traditional method of constructing frame and panel units. You get the strength of mortise-and-tenon joinery and the enhanced appearance of a profile around the inner edge of the frame.

dition, you can offset the groove rather than centering it on the edge. This placement is beneficial if you use a conventional raised panel and want it to be flush.

However, if the sticking is very narrow, you may need to make the groove deeper. In that situation, the groove must extend only from mortise to mortise. Either way, the groove can be cut on the router table.

When you rout the sticking, make several scraps with the profile on one or both edges. You need these to set up the table saw for the next operation.

Now you must miter the sticking so the joints close completely and tightly and you get the crisp right-angle joint between the sticking on the stiles and that on the rails. This is largely a table saw operation.

In preparation, dry-assemble the frame and extend a line from the

shoulder of the sticking on the rail across the face of the stile. When you've marked each joint, disassemble the frame and extend the lines across the outside edges of the stiles.

Begin setting up the saw by attaching a wooden facing to the miter gauge. The facing must be taller than the stiles and rails are wide and long enough to extend beyond the blade. (On my left-tilt saw, I put the miter gauge in the right slot for this operation.) Set a marking gauge to the width of the sticking, and mark parallel to the facing's bottom edge. Trace the mark with a sharp pencil.

Tilt the blade to 45°, and adjust the height to match the sticking. I do this by dropping the blade almost below the table, then kerfing the facing. I raise the blade gradually and kerf the facing after each little adjustment. The goal is to just meet the line established with the marking gauge.

When the height is set, extend a perpendicular reference line from the corner of the kerf to the top edge, as shown in the drawing on the next page.

Test your setup by cutting miters in the sticking scraps.

To miter the sticking on the rails, align the shoulder of the tenon on the vertical reference line on the miter gauge facing. Then snick off the corner of the sticking. To miter the sticking on the stiles, align the sticking width line on the stile with the line on the facing. Make the cut.

The rails are ready for assembly, but the stiles must have the sticking trimmed away from the butt end up to the miter. Do this on the table saw, with the blade set back at 90° and raised as high as possible. Adjust the rip fence so the distance between it and the outside of the blade matches the width of the sticking. Use your scraps to test and confirm the accuracy of the fence setting before you cut the good stuff.

To make the cut, feed the stile into the blade and cut, stopping just shy of the miter. Snap off the sticking, and pare the stile edge smooth with a chisel. (On one end of each stile, you'll be able to see the sticking as you make the cut. On the other end, you'll have to make this cut with the sticking facing down.)

If your cuts are accurate, the sticking on the rail and stile should meet in a tight joint when you assemble the mortise-and-tenon joint.

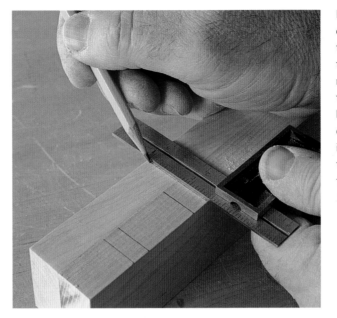

Lay out the mortises on one stile, then transfer the marks to the other. Begin by marking the width of the rail. Inside those lines, mark the width of the sticking, which is one end of the mortise, and the length of the mortise.

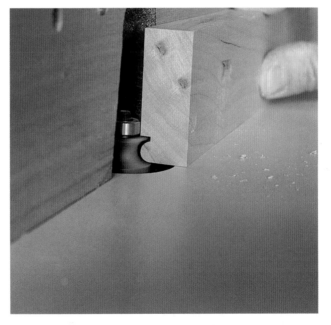

After cutting and fitting the mortise-and-tenon joints, rout the sticking on each rail and stile. One of the benefits of the mitered sticking is that you can use profiles like the quirk-and-bead, which can't be produced with today's cope-and-stick cutters. To cut it, use an edge-beading bit and feed the work through the cut with its face against the router table fence.

Assemble each mortise-and-tenon joint, and at each joint, use a square to extend the shoulder of the sticking from the rail across the face of the stile. Then extend the line across the stile edge. You'll find these lines essential for lining up the stile in the miter gauge for mitering the sticking.

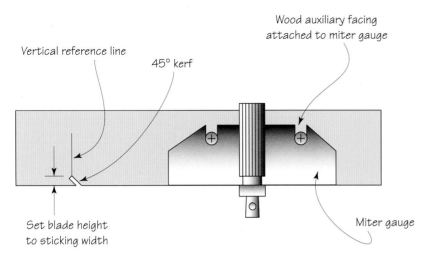

Vertical reference line

45° kerf

Wood auxiliary facing
attached to miter gauge

Set blade height
to sticking width

Miter gauge

Setup for Mitering Sticking

Mitering the sticking on the stiles is where care and accuracy in laying out your reference lines pays off. Align the sticking shoulder line on the stile with the vertical reference line on the miter gauge facing, then cut.

To miter the sticking on the rails, line up the tenon shoulder with the vertical reference line on the miter gauge facing. A quick cut removes the tiny triangle of waste.

A stopped cut on the table saw trims the waste almost completely off the stile. Cut to within 1/4" or so of the miter, with the blade cranked up as high as possible to minimize the cut's arc. The waste then can be snapped free, and the edge can be pared smooth with a chisel.

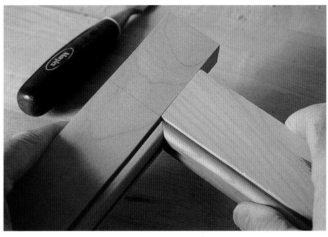

A tight miter joint is the goal. The tenon shoulder must seat tightly against the stile, and the miter of the sticking must also be tight.

Horns

Allow an extra inch of waste on each end of your stiles. After assembly, trim off the excess.

You'll find it easier to assemble the frame if you aren't trying to get the ends of the stiles perfectly flush with the edges of the rails. Scribe pencil lines across the face of stiles where the rails are to align. After the glue dries, you can trim these "horns" and have perfectly flush top and bottom edges.

The extra length allowance began with traditional mortise-and-tenon joinery. Horns make it easier to clamp the stile in a hollow chisel mortiser or a router mortising jig, and they reduce the potential for splitting during mortising or assembly.

Extra length on the end of each stile makes it easier to cut the mortises. The extra bulk prevents the tenon from levering out the end grain between the mortise end and the stile end.

COPE-AND-STICK JOINERY

A happy compromise, cope-and-stick joinery looks attractive and is cut and fit quickly and easily. What it gives up in this bargain is the proven strength of mortise-and-tenon construction.

To make a frame using this joinery, you need a bit or pair of bits and a midpower table-mounted router to drive them. With very little practice, you can set up and cut the joinery for a door in about 15 minutes.

It helps to know about the bits. There are three types on the market, and details on each are in the "Cope-and-Stick Bits" section. You should know both the conventions underlying the joint design and your work-sequence options.

Preparing the Stock

By industry convention, cope-and-stick bits are designed for $3/4$"-thick stock. Because this stock thickness is standard in most areas of the United States and Canada, you shouldn't have problems if you buy dressed stock.

You do have some leeway, however. The typical sticking bit produces a $5/8$" cut, leaving a $1/8$"-thick shoulder to the panel groove. You can finesse the bit height setting to either reduce the profile width and increase the shoulder width, or to increase the profile and reduce the shoulder. The problem when you creep below $11/16$" in thickness is in fitting the sticking profile on the edge and still having enough stock to support the panel groove. As the thickness creeps above $7/8$", the capacity of the cope cutter becomes a problem. You probably will find the cutter leaves a wafer of waste attached at the end edge of the rail.

The usual caveats about your stock apply: Use defect-free, straight-grained lumber.

I know, I know — we usually take such provisos with a grain of salt, and you can get away with using slightly bowed stock for a frame and panel

Able to be cut quickly with special router bits (or shaper cutters), the cope-and-stick joint is the standard for cabinet doors. Properly fitted and glued, it is a strong, enduring joint, despite what traditionalists often claim.

unit, so long as it isn't a door. If the wood in a frame and panel unit is bowed, the unit will be bowed. If the unit is a structural part of a case, it will be anchored to other elements that will pull it into line and hold it there. But if it is a door, it won't hang flat — that you won't be able to conceal.

So for doors especially, the stock must be flat, straight and true.

Dress the chosen stock to whatever thickness you settle on. You ought to have some extra stock so you can make a replacement for any rail or stile that you make a mistake on along the way. You also need several pieces for testing the setups; bear in mind that these particular pieces can be a secondary wood. The important thing is to plane all the stock to a consistent thickness. I achieve consistency by planing all of it at the same time.

Rip the stock to width, then cross-cut the parts to length. When you cut the rails, you have to account for the profile width. For example, if you are making an 18"-wide door and using $1\frac{3}{4}$"-wide stiles, the distance between the stiles is $14\frac{1}{2}$". The rails must be longer than that in order to overlap the sticking profile. If the profile is $\frac{3}{8}$" wide, then you need to add $\frac{3}{4}$" to the length of the rails ($\frac{3}{8}$" for each stile, or twice the width of the profile). Although this may be awkward to verbalize, it is quite easy to visualize; see the drawing "Determining Rail Length."

Typical Dimensions

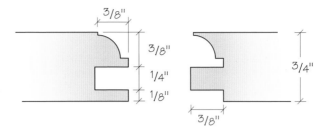

Determining Rail Length

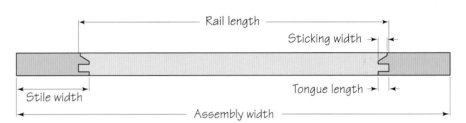

To determine the rail length, subtract the width of both stiles from the assembly width, then add twice the tongue width. The sticking width is not always equal to the tongue length.

Typically, to determine the rail length, you subtract the width of both stiles from the assembly width, then add twice the sticking width. However, be sure the sticking width equals the length of the tongue.

COPE-AND-STICK BITS

Cope-and-stick frame joinery can be cut with any of three styles of router bits.

Two-Bit Set

The most common style is the two-bit set. Here you have a sticking bit, which does the groove and profile, and a separate cope bit, which forms the stub tenon and the cope.

Typically, the profile cutter is an integral part of the shank, while the bearing and the slotting cutter are separate parts, secured on an arbor projecting from the bit. The sticking cutter has a bearing mounted on the tip, so it can be used to make curved cuts, as is required to make arched rails. The cope bit has the bearing mounted between the profile cutter and the groover. Usually, the bits come all set up to produce a properly fitted joint. It'll be a slip fit, not particularly tight. The logic is that glue will swell the wood, and when swollen with glue, the fit will be just right.

A few makers include two or three shims with the bits to give you a little control over the fit. (Most often, the shims become useful after the bits have been resharpened a time or two.) You use the shims to alter the thickness of the tenon. To tighten the joint's fit, add a shim or two between the two cutters on the cope bit's arbor, thus increasing the tenon thickness. To loosen the fit, remove shims from that location.

A slightly different — and cheaper — version of the two-bit set integrates the profile and slot cutters into the bit body. There's a bearing on the tip of both bits in the set, but it's positioned to work against a template, not the work itself. For straight cuts, the bit must be used with a fence. The advantage of this design is that you can readily work stock up to 1" thick. The disadvantages are that you must use a template to make curved sticking cuts and you can't adjust the fit of the joint, even after the bit's been resharpened.

Using two-bit set is the most common way to cut cope-and-stick joinery. The decorative profile and the panel groove, collectively known as the sticking, are formed in one pass using the sticking bit (resting on the tabletop). The cope cutter — in the router collet — machines the stub tenon and profile cope on the ends of the rails and muntins.

The overall advantage of the two-bit set is that you don't have to break down the bit to switch from one cut to the other. For those who do lots of frame and panel work, this means that two routers can be set up, one for each bit. This makes the switch from sticking to coping even easier.

Reversible Assembly

A less expensive — and probably less convenient — bit is the reversible assembly. You get an arbor with an integral shank, a bearing and separate profile and slot cutters. Instead of swapping bits to switch from sticking to coping, you switch the positions of the cutters on the arbor. To make the cope cut, you put the slot cutter on the bottom, then the bearing and finally the profile cutter. For the sticking cut, the profile cutter is on the bottom, topped by the slot cutter and the bearing. This may not be the right match for you if you're at all random or the least bit fumble fingered.

Some reversible bits come with brass shims you use to adjust the fit of the joint, especially after the cutters

have been resharpened a time or two.

This kind of bit harbors a "gotcha!" or two. One is in the swapping of cutters. Don't turn over either one. The router spins only one direction; when it is mounted in a table, you see the bit turn counterclockwise. If you inadvertently flip over the cutters (which is easiest to do with the slotting cut; the profile cutter always faces up), the cutting tips will face the wrong way and the bit won't cut. (Smoke? Yes, but not cut.) The second "gotcha!" is the workpiece orientation. With a matched set, the bits are configured so the workpiece orientation is the same (usually facedown) for both cope and sticking cuts. With a reversible assembly, you cut the sticking with the face down, but you do the copes with the face up.

The advantage of the reversible assembly — the cost difference aside — is the perfectly matched cuts it yields. Because you use the same cutters to produce both cope and sticking cuts, they're guaranteed to match. The disadvantage, of course, is that you have to dismantle the bit when switching from one cut to the other.

The reversible bit produces both the sticking and cope cuts. The appearance of the cuts and the strength of the joint equal those produced by two-bit sets. The reversible bit is generally less expensive but somewhat more onerous to use.

The reversible bit's onerousness stems from the need to rearrange the cutters on the arbor when alternating between cope cuts and sticking cuts. The typical assembly consists of an arbor (in the router collet here), a profile cutter (top left), a slotting cutter (bottom left), some shims (on the slotting cutter), a pilot bearing and a nut. You supply the wrench.

To set up a reversible bit for a cope cut, drop the slotting cutter onto the arbor (making sure the cutting tips are oriented to cut on a counterclockwise rotation). Then add the bearing; shims, as necessary; the profile cutter; and, finally, the nut to secure everything.

For a sticking cut, drop the profile cutter onto the arbor first. Then add shims as necessary, and the slotting cutter. The bearing and nut go on last.

Stacked Bit

The third style is the stacked bit. This is a single bit with both cope and stick cutters on the same body. The least expensive versions have the cutting edges laid out in as compact a way as possible, so you have that face up vs. face down "gotcha!" to look out for. This version has a single bearing.

Top-of-the-line versions eliminate the "gotcha!"; the payback is a considerably larger bit and two bearings (one above the cutters, one below). With some brands, you orient the work face down; with others, face up.

Most cope-and-stick cutters, of whatever style, are $1\frac{1}{2}$" in diameter. Those high-end stackers are massive bits, however, as much as 2" in diameter and 4" tall, overall.

Any of the three bit types will cut the frame joinery just fine. You should be able to choose from several profiles — typically an ogee profile, a quarter-round profile or a bead. Some bit manufacturers have an even grander assortment.

You may find cope-and-stick cutters on $\frac{1}{4}$" shanks. Don't waste your money on them. Buy these bits on $\frac{1}{2}$"-shanks only.

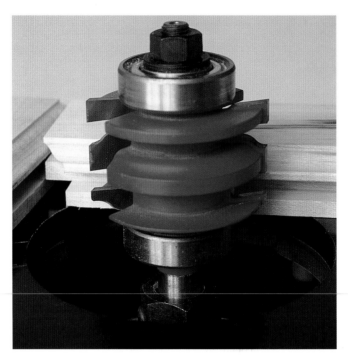

The stacked cope-and-stick bit tends to be bulky because it has both cutting profiles and two bearings on a single shank. Nevertheless, it can be powered by a midsize router running flat out. It produces the same cuts as matched pairs but requires a little less setup because you merely raise or lower the router to switch from one cut to the other.

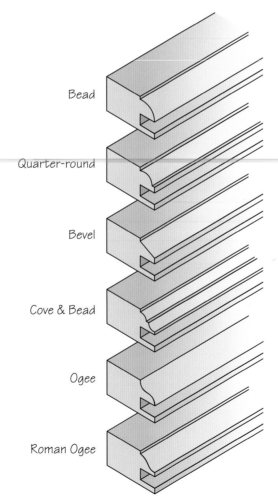

Bead

Quarter-round

Bevel

Cove & Bead

Ogee

Roman Ogee

Common Sticking Profiles

CUTTING THE JOINERY

If you have just purchased a bit or set of bits to do cope-and-stick joinery, you should spend a little time getting familiar with it. Take as much time as you need to make both cope and sticking cuts. Here's your goal: a setup block (see Setup Block later in this chapter) with an edge sticked and an end coped. With that in hand, you can quickly set up the bits any time you need to.

The usual routine is to cope the rail ends first, then stick all the stiles and rails.

Cope the Rail Ends

Before doing any setup or cuts, reflect on the fact that the cope cut is a cross-grained cut. That means you need to back up the work to prevent splinters from being torn from the back edge by the cutter. Depending on the size and number of rails, I usually gang them up and feed the lot of them past the cutter, pushing them along the fence with a square scrap. That pusher acts as a backup, preventing the splintering.

Some woodworkers prefer to use a more formal guide, like the coping sled, and to cope the rails one at a time. No shame in that at all. I bring this up now because the sled does impact the bit-height setting: You have to accommodate the sled base's thickness.

The first task in setup, of course, is preparing the bit. Place the cope cutter in the router's collet. To do this, you'll probably shift the fence back from the bit opening in the tabletop. If you are using an assembly-type bit, you may need to switch the positions of the cutters on the bit arbor.

Once the bit is secured in the collet, establish a height setting using your setup block. You can tuck it into the bit

and adjust the bit up and down. If you use a coping sled, you must set the block on the sled when gauging the bit elevation.

Set the fence next, positioning it with the face tangent to the pilot bearing. House the bit in the fence as much as possible for the safest operation. In addition, the more closely matched the

fence opening is to the bit contour, the better the fence will back up the cut. If your fence has a split facing, simply shift the two fence elements toward the bit until they nearly touch it, then lock them down. On my router table, I mount a plywood, hardboard or MDF facing to the fence with a bit opening customized to the bit being used.

Setting the height of the coping bit is easy if you have a setup block, either one you've produced yourself while making some test cuts, or one supplied with the bits. You should be able to slide the block on and off the cutter. If the cutter pinches the block against the tabletop, the cutter is too low; if it lifts the block off the tabletop, it's too high.

The face of the fence must be tangent to the bit's pilot bearing. Lock down one end of the fence, and swing the free end fractionally as you slide a straightedge back and forth across the fence and bearing. Your straightedge should graze the bearing without turning it.

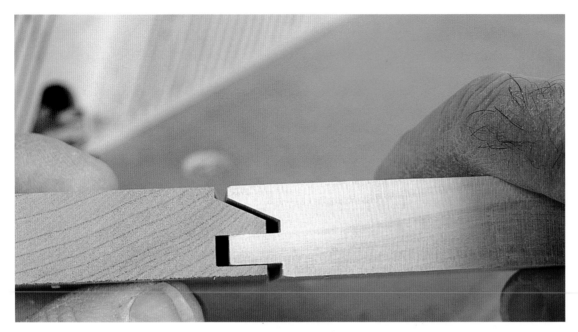

Make a test-cut in scrap material of exactly the same thickness as the rail and stile stock. Fit the test-cut to your setup block and assess the fit. The faces of the two parts should be flush, and the profiles should fit together tightly. If needed, adjust the bit height or the fence position, then make another test-cut.

Set the hold-downs next. Use a featherboard or two to keep the work tight to the tabletop. Position them just fore and aft of the bit, where you need the pressure.

Of course you need to make a test cut. Fit the test piece to the setup block's sticked edge. If necessary, adjust the bit up or down to get the surfaces flush.

With your setup tested, you are ready to cut.

The cope cuts should be completed in one pass. Repeating a pass can enlarge the cut and create a loose fit. In theory, a second pass can enlarge the cut only if there's some movement in your setup. In practice, there probably is a skosh of movement possible no matter how stiff your featherboards and how firmly you grip the work.

Pay attention when you turn the rails to cope the second end. You should turn them, not flip them. Mark the face that's supposed to be up as you make the cope cut. Before you cut, look for the mark.

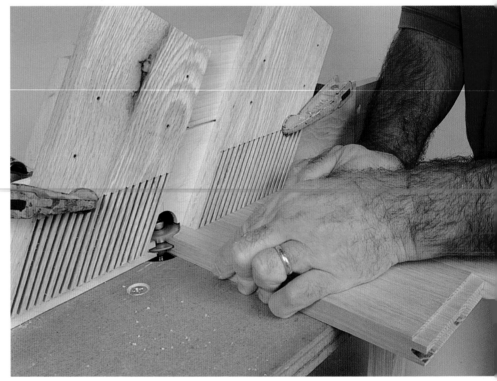

Once the setup is dialed in, rout the copes on the ends of the rails. I don't usually use a coping sled. Ganging up a brace of rails and a wide backup helps keep the rail ends square against the fence, and it expedites the work to boot. The tandem featherboards, positioned so the direct pressure is not on the bit but on either side of it, help keep the work against the tabletop.

Making a Coping Sled

Prefer to guide your cope cuts with a device more "formal" than a scrap block of wood? What you need is a coping sled.

This simple sled is used in conjunction with the fence. That is, there's no slide for a miter gauge slot. Instead, the sled is pushed against the fence at the same time it is advanced along the fence.

The construction is evident in the drawing.

A couple of construction notes: I recommend that the base be $\frac{1}{2}$"-thick material because that provides a better backing for the toggle clamp. I know I have a propensity to want that clamp to snap, making me feel it is holding the work tightly. Maybe you will too. The workpiece in turn is being pressed with great force against the base. If the base is thin and bendy, it'll distort and you won't get consistent, accurate cuts with the sled.

The handgrip can be a block of wood, a fat dowel, a turned shape or, as shown, a copy of a hand plane's tote. I cocked the tote at an angle, so when I push, I apply pressure toward the fence as well as along it.

The sled's backup fence will be cut by the cope bit the first time you use it. On the plus side, this allows you to use the sled to set the cope bit's height.

On the negative side, it behooves you to make a different sled for each different cope-and-stick set you use. Otherwise you'll get tear-out as the bit exits the work and cuts into the sled, and the sticking cut will remove that tear-out at only one end of the rail.

An alternative is to use a separate backup strip between the sled's fence and the rail. Hold it in place with carpet tape.

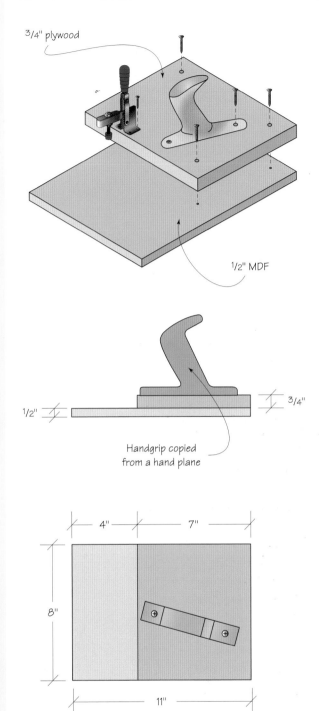

3/4" plywood

1/2" MDF

1/2"   3/4"

Handgrip copied
from a hand plane

4"   7"

8"

11"

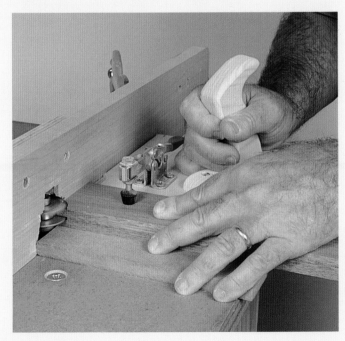

A coping sled holds the rail securely for the cut and provides some backup against tear-out. It gives you a comfortable, sure grip on the work and keeps your hand out of the bit's way. A trade-off is that the bit has to be extended an extra $\frac{1}{2}$" above the tabletop, which isn't a simple matter on every router table.

Cope and Rip

Coping the ends of rails individually can sometimes be discouraging. From time to time, you discover the shoulders of the cuts are wavy because the rails weren't as well secured in your coping sled as you thought. Your stock can split out at the end of a cut.

A timesaving way to lick these problems is to cope the ends of wide boards, then rip them to the widths required for the rails. A wide board is much easier to guide along the fence than a narrow one, and one wide board is easier to manage than four rails butted edge to edge. I have a friend who will go so far as to edge-glue stock just so he can cut the copes this way.

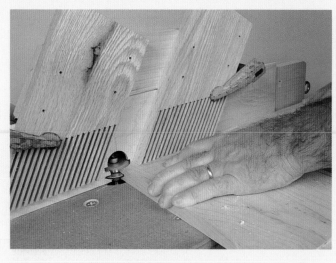

The wider a board is, the easier it is to keep square to the fence. To get clean, straight shoulders on your cope cuts, a workable approach is to cope the ends of a piece of stock that's wide enough to yield two or more rails.

After the copes are cut, rip the board into rails. The number of steps necessary remains the same; just the order changes.

Coping Sticked Rails

From time to time, you get into this situation: You've already made the sticking cuts, but you haven't done the cope cuts. Each rail is now a candidate for an end-of-cut blowout that will spoil its appearance.

Here's a remedy: As soon as the coping bit is set up, plow a cut along the edge of a strip of extra stock. Tuck this strip into the sticking cut on the rail, its end flush with the rail's end. Now the sticking is backed up for that cross-grained cope cut.

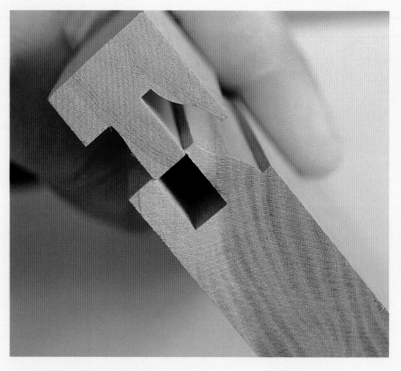

The only problem with routing the sticking on rails before doing the cope cuts is the possibility of tear-out. You're almost assured of getting it on one end of each rail, and it will deface the work. But if you cut the cope profile on a scrap strip, you can tuck it into the sticking of the rail. This will back up the sticking and prevent tear-out.

Rout the Sticking

Chuck the sticking bit in the router collet and adjust its height. To do this, you'll have to shift the fence out of the way. Make an initial adjustment using your setup block. After the fence and featherboards are reset, you can make a test-cut. Fit your test piece to one of the coped rails; chances are, if you set the bit carefully with the precut block, you'll be dead on. If some adjustment is necessary, make it and run a new test piece across the bit. Keep adjusting and testing until you have the fit you want.

Reposition the fence after making the initial bit adjustment; set it so its facing is tangent to the bit's pilot bearing. The bit opening should be as close around the bit as possible. While this won't completely eliminate chipping ahead of the cutter, it will minimize it. The opening that accommodated the cope bit surely will fit the sticking bit.

Reset your featherboard hold-downs next. Use these to keep the work tight to the tabletop. Position them just fore and aft of the bit, where you need the pressure.

When everything is set up properly, make a test-cut, then make whatever adjustments are needed. When the setting is just right, rout the sticking on all the stiles and rails. One pass should be sufficient to complete each cut.

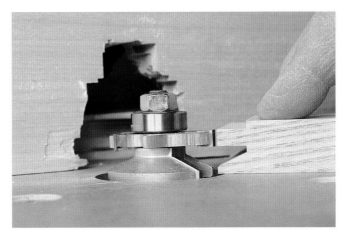

Here's one of two practical ways to set the height of the sticking bit. Use a coped rail and adjust the bit's slotter cutter to align with the stub tenon.

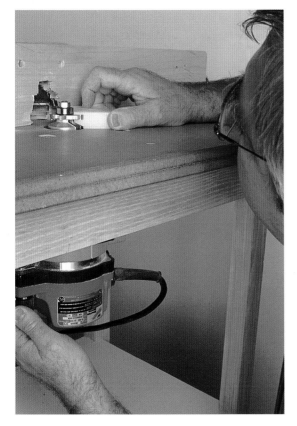

Another practical way to adjust the sticking bit height is with a setup block. Here I'm using a plastic block provided with the bits by the manufacturer. I hunker down so I can sight across the tabletop to the bit. From this position, it's convenient to reach under the table to adjust the router.

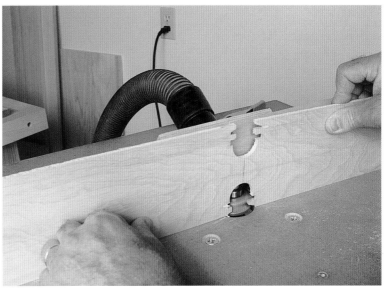

Use a thin hardboard or plywood facing for the fence, and cut a zero-clearance opening for the bit. Cut an initial opening for the bearing and arbor. Press the outfeed side against the fence, but flex the rest of the plywood and hold it clear of the bit. Switch on the router, and roll the facing onto the fence while the bit cuts through the edges of the opening. Then secure the facing with carpet tape or spring clamps.

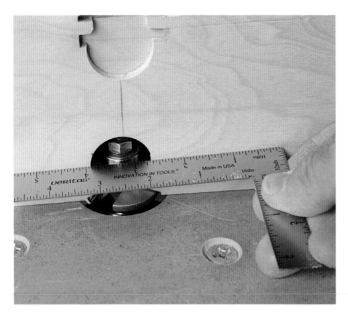

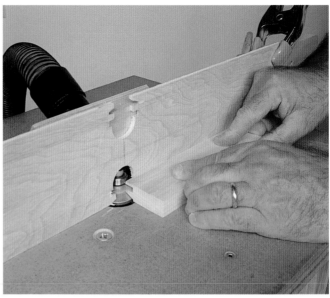

Position the fence tangent to the bit's pilot bearing. Use a straight-edge or small rule that spans the bit opening to set the fence. Slide the rule across the opening; if it contacts and turns the bearing, shift the fence until the rule is just clear of the bearing.

Before setting the featherboards, I usually make a test-cut. Use a short piece of the working stock for this.

Check the fit of this test-cut to the cope on a rail. The goal is flush faces and a full-depth sticking cut, as is the case here.

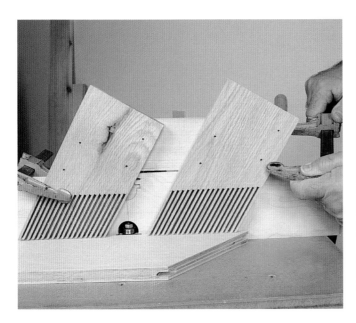

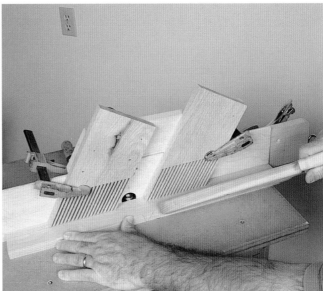

With the fence and bit all set, clamp featherboards to the fence to help control the workpieces as you feed them through the cut. I use a tandem featherboard, which is simply two separate featherboards joined in parallel with a cleat. The featherboards are positioned with the bit in the gap between them. I use a scrap of $^3/_4$"-thick plywood as a spacer to set the featherboards because it's about $^1/_{32}$" thinner than my frame stock. That translates into firm but not excessive featherboard pressure.

Routing the sticking is a straightforward operation at this point. Although you can feed each stick through the cut with your hands, most woodworkers are more comfortable using a pusher. Mine has a V groove in the bottom edge and a heel at the end to catch the end of the workpiece. Pushing thus forces the workpiece against the fence as well as through the cut. The featherboards keep the work against the tabletop and shield the bit as well.

Once the rails are coped and all the parts are sticked, the frame is ready for the panels.

Dealing with Chipping

It's a knife in the heart: The sticking profile you've just cut along the edge is all chipped.

There isn't much you can do to salvage that piece, but you might be able to prevent such chipping in the rest of the run.

First, look over your stock to see if you can work a different edge. Chipping along the edge of the profile is usually a result of susceptible wood colliding with a delicate profile and an aggressive feed. By "susceptible wood" I mean boards with gnarly, swirling, undulating grain that runs off the edge to be worked. Even boards with fairly straight grain that happens to run off the working edge can be prone to chipping.

Examine your fence to see if you can create more of a zero-clearance opening for the bit. A little more back-up for the stock can be helpful.

Finally, rout the sticking in two or more passes. Working a board with a sticking profile that, when combined with the panel groove, produces something akin to a knife edge is asking for serious chipping. Move the fence forward, housing more of the bit and limiting the cut. Make a shallow first cut, then shift the fence for a deep second pass. Clean up with a very light final pass.

Don't consider climb-cutting. Though climb-cutting can sometimes be a solution in a handheld-router operation, it is always extremely high risk on the router table.

If you make an aggressive cut with a sticking profile that tapers to a delicate edge, especially on a board with gnarly grain at the edge, the result just might be disappointing. Chipping has ruined this piece, but you can take some measures — including tempering your aggression — to reduce or eliminate chipping on your next piece.

Avoid Splintering

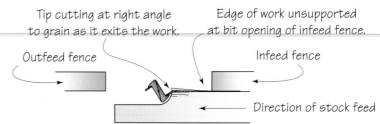

Tip cutting at right angle to grain as it exits the work.

Edge of work unsupported at bit opening of infeed fence.

Outfeed fence

Infeed fence

Direction of stock feed

Splintering occurs when the fence opening is larger than the bit, leaving a gap between the cutting edges and the infeed fence's surface.

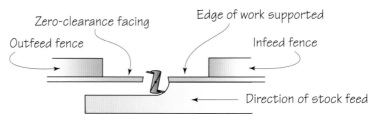

Zero-clearance facing

Edge of work supported

Outfeed fence

Infeed fence

Direction of stock feed

Add zero-clearance facing to each fence to support the work right up to the bit.

Top Views

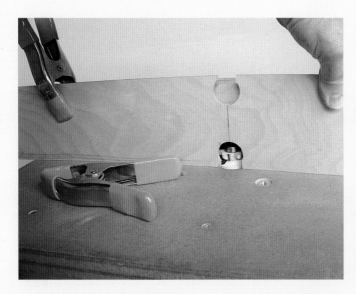

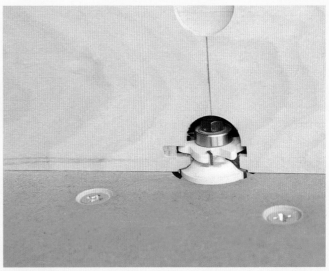

Thin plywood (or hardboard) makes an excellent zero-clearance facing for the fence. I usually have usable scraps of it, so in effect it's free and disposable. Cut a strip 3" to 4" wide and as long as the fence. Use a Forstner bit to bore 1"-diameter (or larger) holes in the plywood near both the top and bottom edges, then use a band saw to open the holes. This opening is bigger than the bearing but smaller than the bit. Secure the facing to the fence with spring clamps or carpet tape.

To cut the zero-clearance profile, you can swing one end of the fence so the bit is inside. Switch on the router, and slowly swing the fence, allowing the bit to cut through the facing. Don't fret about splintering in this facing at the outfeed side of the bit; that's inevitable. Pick away any chips that will impede the movement of the work. The infeed side is where the zero-clearance is needed.

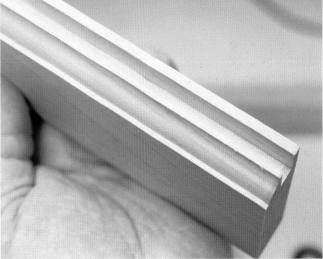

To further reduce the chances of chipping, make the first pass a scoring cut, in other words, one that's very shallow. This pass will define the shoulders of the panel groove and the margin of the profile.

The result of these measures — a zero-clearance facing, an initial scoring cut and perhaps an intermediate cut before a light final pass — will be a clean, crisp, chip-free cut.

Setup Block

Take the guesswork out of setting up your cope-and-stick cutters by making a setup block. Not only does a setup block help you set the bit elevations without a lot of test cuts and fine tuning, it also puts you in control of the appearance of the finished joints.

From an aesthetic viewpoint, the sticking cut is paramount because it establishes the appearance of the joinery. Operationally, though, the sticking usually is cut after the rails have been coped. Unfortunately, doing the copes first pretty much consigns you to accepting whatever appearance you get for the sticking. The two cuts do have to match.

A setup block solves that problem.

Make sticking cuts on sample stock, experimenting with the bit elevation. When you have a setting that's optimum to your eye, mark it and set it aside.

Switch cutters and rout some copes, fitting them to your sample with the optimum sticking profile. When you have the perfect fit, cope one end of the piece with the optimum sticking cut. Now you have one piece of wood with optimum profiles that are perfectly matched to each other.

Trim the block to a tidy size for storage with your bits. For the next project, you can set the cope cutter quickly by using the setup block, and you'll know you won't be disappointed by the appearance of your finished assemblies.

A setup block can take the worry out of making the critical bit-height settings, especially for woodworkers who don't do the job frequently. For my pair of Amana bits, which aren't supplied with setup blocks, I made a setup block that's essentially a short piece of a rail. The end is coped and the edge is sticked.

REINFORCING COPE-AND-STICK JOINERY

Loose tenons are a great way to reinforce cope-and-stick joints. Cut by a pair of matched cutters, these clever joints are quick and easy to make and look great, but they aren't tremendously strong. With loose tenons, you can transform them into mortise-and-tenon joints.

To do this, cut mortises into both halves of the joint, and, at assembly, insert a separate strip of wood as a tenon. This means there's no tenon to work around as you cut the copes and the sticking.

Rout the mortises before coping the rail ends and sticking the edges. To avoid having the panel groove cut into the mortises, offset the mortises $^9/_{16}$" or so from the inner edges of the rails and locate the edge mortises in the stiles accordingly.

When you stick the rails, be mindful of this offset. I have found it all too easy to rout the profile and panel groove into the wrong edge.

Center the mortises across the edges. They won't align with the stub tenon produced by the cope cut, but that doesn't matter. The tenon isn't going to show in the assembled joint.

Although cope-and-stick joinery is satisfactory for most frame and panel constructions, reinforcing the joints with dowels or loose tenons (shown) is never a bad idea. The larger the construction, the more beneficial the reinforcement.

Mortises for loose tenons can be cut in a variety of ways. I use this shop-made mortising block (plans for it are in *Bill Hylton's Power-Tool Joinery*), which has interchangeable horizontal and vertical workrests. Use the former for routing edge mortises (in stiles) and the latter for end mortises (in rails). The cutting is done with an ordinary plunge router fitted with an edge guide.

Locating End Mortises

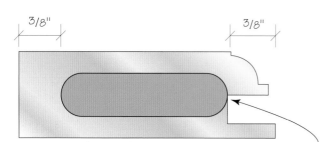

If the end mortise is
equidistant from the edges
it conflicts with
the panel groove.

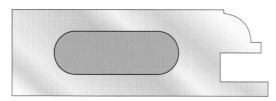

Offset the mortise more from the
sticked edge than from
the outside edge.

To rout the mortises in the edges of the stile, set up the mortising block with the horizontal workrest in place and adjusted to bring the top edge of the stile flush with the top of the block. Align the mortise center line with the block's setup line (the red one) and clamp the stile with the toggles. The router's edge guide positions the bit for the cut: the stops limit the lateral movement of the router, thus establishing the mortise length.

A good way to ensure the mortise and the panel groove won't intersect in the rails is to lay out the mortise on the end of a sticked sample (inset). You can then use it to set up the vertical workrest on the mortising block, as shown. Line up the mortise center line with the setup line on the block and clamp the sample. Then slide the workrest against the sample and secure it. Orient the sticked edge so it will be against the workrest.

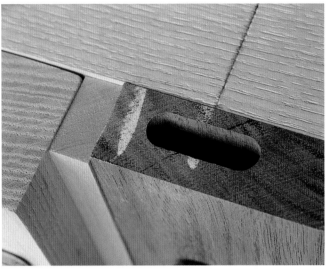

To ensure all the mortises align, orient each workpiece with the same face against the block. Because the end mortises in the rails are offset from the edge to be sticked, you must use a shim or spacer to position the piece for each cut. One mortise in each rail is routed without the shim (right) and one with the shim (left). The chalk marks indicate roughly where the mortise should be.

The coping and sticking cuts are made without interference from the mortises. Mill a strip of stock to fit the mortises and round the edges, then crosscut individual tenons.

GROOVE-AND-STUB-TENON JOINERY

A quick and easy kin to cope-and-stick joinery is the groove-and-stub-tenon joint. You can do all the joinery cuts with one bit, either a straight bit or a slotting cutter. You don't get a high-style assembly or the strength of a mortise-and-tenon assembly, but you do get a utilitarian assembly for doors, web frames and even casework.

Because the stub tenons will be centered on the stock, the groove should be centered also. But you should cut the groove first, then fit the tenon to it. The easiest way to cut the groove and be sure it is centered is, of course, to make two passes. Using a slotting cutter? Make one pass with the face down on the table and the other with the back down. With a straight bit, orient the face against the fence for one pass and the back against it for the other.

Either way, the groove becomes wider than the bit. This should not be a problem. Use a $3/16$" cutter if a $1/4$"-wide groove is essential. In most cases a groove that's $5/16$" or $3/8$" wide isn't bad. You don't have a profile to fit on the edge. The tenons haven't been cut, and a thicker tenon is likely to be a stronger tenon.

The flip side is that this joinery makes the use of $1/4$"-thick plywood for the panels easier to accommodate. You simply cut a groove that's less than $1/4$" wide (something you can't do with most cope-and-stick cutters). Here you would use a $1/8$" or $3/16$" slotting cutter, for example.

With the frame parts grooved, cut the tenons. Lower the slotting cutter so it cuts the bottom surface of the rail (rather than the top surface). Adjust the fence so a straight bit is cutting on the face that's against the fence. Creep up on the fit.

Groove-and-stub-tenon joinery is a great choice for utilitarian constructions, like this shop-cabinet door. This joinery, remarkably similar to cope-and-stick joinery, is actually better at accommodating $1/4$"-thick plywood panels because it's easy to produce a panel groove less than $1/4$" wide. That panel can be glued in place, thus reinforcing the entire construction.

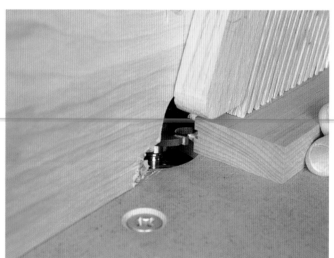

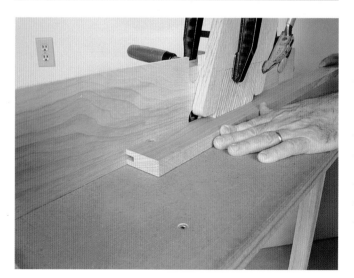

Even if the frame is utilitarian, you probably don't want your work marred by chipping along the edges of the panel grooves. Make the first pass a shallow scoring cut. Set the fence to expose only the tips of the slotting cutter for this pass (top left). After all the pieces are scored, reset the fence tangent to the bearing, and make a full-depth cut (bottom left). The featherboard, incidentally, is clamped to the fence, so it will ride along when you reposition the fence to deepen the groove.

Because the panel groove is less than $1/4$" wide to accommodate a plywood panel, the shoulder cuts that form the tenon must be more than $1/4$" wide. Add a second slotting cutter to the arbor so those cuts can be made in one pass. Be sure to place the bearing on top to simplify setting the fence.

Use a grooved workpiece to set the bit height for the tenoning cuts. The cuts should transpire at tabletop level, not above the tenon. After resetting the fence, cut a sample tenon to confirm your height adjustment.

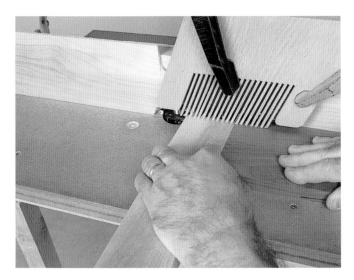

Each tenon is formed in two passes. The featherboard keeps the work flat on the tabletop; a push block — just a square scrap — helps keep the rail end square to the fence and also minimizes tear-out.

The stub tenon may look a bit slim, but the groove-and-stub-tenon joint is plenty strong for applications like web frames and cabinet doors. This groove is narrow specifically because it's for a plywood panel, which will be glued in place. For a thicker panel, cut a wider groove and a thicker tenon.

MITERED HALF LAP

If you like the look of a crisp miter, try making door frames with mitered half laps. These joints are strong yet easy to rout, and they allow you to rout a profile on the inside edge before assembly. After assembly, the profile meets at the miter.

Half-lap joints in general — T-laps, end laps and cross laps, in addition to mitered half laps — can be used for all sorts of flat frames: doors, of course, but also face frames, web frames and frames for frame and panel casework. An intermediate rail half-lapped to the stiles "looks" right because it visually abuts the stile (the way a mortise and tenon would) rather than crossing it (the way a bridle joint would). On the other hand, a rectangle of end grain is exposed in assembled end laps and T-laps, which can be regarded as unsightly.

Despite its simplicity, a half-lap joint can be very strong if made properly. The shoulder(s) of the half-lap joints provide resistance to twisting. In addition, the laps provide plenty of long-grain surface to be glued.

The mitered half lap combines the structure of the half-lap joint with the appearance of the miter joint. Of course, you can't just miter two pieces that have already been half-lapped. One part of the joint could be done this way: On the rails the shoulder cut is square, whereas the butt end is mitered. On the stiles, the shoulder cut is mitered, but the butt end is square.

What you need is a set of three guides: right-hand and left-hand miter guides and a right-angle guide. Make them from sheets of MDF or plywood and strips of hardwood. Use a bit — either straight or mortising — with a shank-mounted bearing to cut the joinery. No such bits in your collection? Add router fences to the top of the guides and use a regular straight bit.

Make the Guides

Cut three bases to the same dimensions — 7" × 13" — and be sure their corners are absolutely square. (Choose the thickness of the material you use based on the length of the bit you intend to use. A $\frac{3}{4}$" thickness will ensure that the bearing of a 1" pattern bit — a common size — will have a reference surface without having to cut too deeply in the work.)

Attach the fences, then cut a 45° miter across two of the templates. Be sure you locate the fences and cut the miters to create right and left templates, *not* duplicates.

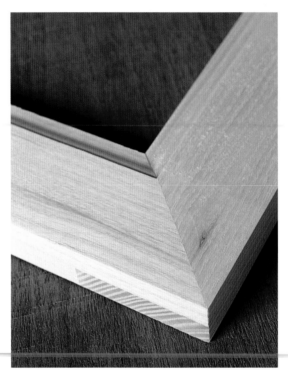

A crisp, tight miter gives a slightly different look to the half lap. The mitered half lap is strong yet easy to make, and it allows you to rout a profile on the inside edge before assembly. After assembly, the profiles will meet at the miter. Only the strips of end grain on the top and bottom edges of the assembled frame expose the joint as something other than a regular miter.

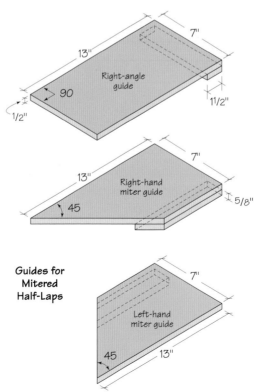

Guides for Mitered Half-Laps

Cutting the Laps

Begin by machining the workpieces and trimming the pieces to final length. Miter the ends of the rails, and cut the ends of the stiles square.

You can cut a groove or rabbet for the panel before or after cutting the joinery; I prefer to do it afterward. The same is true of the profile. Cut it before lapping or cut it after; I prefer after.

The rails are lapped across their backs. To ensure they're identical, cut both laps at the same time, using the right-angle guide. Butt them edge to edge, faces down, and clamp them together. Set the guide in place, its reference edge right on the shoulder line. Clamp it, set the router's depth of cut and have at it.

With the rails done, turn to the stiles. The stiles are lap-cut across their faces. Clamp the appropriate guide to each piece and, with the router setting unchanged, rout each lap. Repeat until all laps are cut.

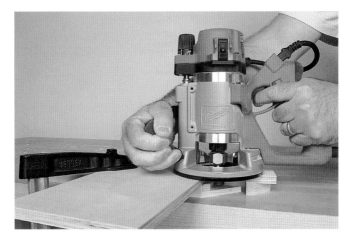

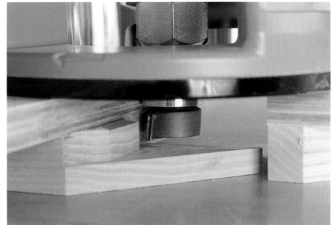

The right-angle guide is used to guide the router to cut the laps into the rails, which are mitered. You can do them one at a time or put both rails together. Align the guide exactly on the shoulder. To avoid splintering, feed the cutter into the workpiece from all sides. Note the support block — a scrap of the guide's base plus a scrap of the frame stock fastened together — which is secured with carpet tape to the router base.

The stiles have square ends, so the angle guides must be used to rout the laps on them. A right-hand angle guide is used on one end and a left-hand guide is used on the other; you can clamp both to a stile and cut one end, then the other.

Because the mitered half lap has a square shoulder as well as a miter, clamps set parallel to the members allow you to close the joints tightly. To ensure the cheeks of the laps bond properly, apply a spring clamp or small hand clamp to each joint.

ASSEMBLY

Assembling a frame around a panel is pretty straightforward. At the end of the process, you should have a unit that's square, flat and true. The frame's members should be joined together securely, and the panel should float freely in its grooves.

To ensure you achieve your goals:

• Work on a flat, true surface. This is essential if the final assembly is to be flat and true.

• Assemble the parts without glue, going so far as to tighten the clamps and check the diagonal measurements. You do this to demonstrate that the parts do go together. If there's a problem with fit, it's better to know about it *before* glue is spread.

• Finish the panel, right down to a coat of wax. This step has several benefits. The finish and wax will prevent glue squeeze-out from bonding the panel to the frame. It will ensure that finish doesn't bond it to the frame. It will eliminate the possibility of shrinkage, which exposes slivers of bare wood at the margins of the panel.

For the setup, position a pair of bar or pipe clamps with the jaws adjusted just a bit wider than the assembly. Have your glue and a small brush at hand, along with a wet rag for cleaning up squeeze-out.

Apply glue judiciously to the ends of a rail (it is easiest to apply to both ends while you hold the rail in your hand). Join it to a stile. If you've already trimmed the stiles to their final length, you must keep the rail's edge aligned with the stile's end.

Slip the panel into the groove. Don't glue it. Remember, it needs to float. Lay this partial assembly on the clamp bars.

Apply glue to the ends of the second rail, and add it to the assembly. Tip up the assembly, and fit the second stile into place. Align the parts, and lower the assembly onto the clamp bars. The rails should rest on the clamp bars

with the jaws square to the stile edges. Tighten the clamps gently, alternating back and forth between the clamps and keeping the rails flat on the clamp bars. As the joints close, stop. Very little pressure is required, and overtightening the clamps will likely distort the joints and, thus, the assembly.

Now make sure the assembly is square. To do this, measure the diagonals; they should be the same. If they aren't, the assembly is not square; loosen the clamps some, and square the assembly by tapping at the corners of the longer diagonal. If this gentle persuasion doesn't do the trick, apply a clamp across those corners. As you very slowly tighten the clamp, monitor the length of the opposite diagonal (the shorter one). When the difference between the diagonal measurements is

gone, stop. Retighten the clamps across the assembly and recheck the diagonal measurements.

Next, make sure the assembly is flat. Lay a straightedge across the frame and panel and check at several places from stile to stile, then from rail to rail, then diagonally. If the assembly isn't flat, loosen the clamps and push the frame down against the clamp bars. As you retighten the clamps, remember not to overtighten them.

Now clean up the squeeze-out. Use a wet rag wrapped around the tip of a pencil, knife blade or chisel to get the inside corners clean. Even though the moisture in the wet rag will raise the grain, it's a lot easier to sand raised grain smooth than it is to scrape off dried glue.

Assembling a cope-and-stick construction is straightforward but not without the occasional "gotcha!" (see chapter 3 "Making Panels"). Eliminate an obvious gotcha by completely finishing the panel before assembly. Glue that squeezes into the corners of the panel groove from the frame joinery is less likely to stick to a finished, waxed surface.

Use a small brush to apply glue. For some assemblies, a bead of glue straight out of the bottle is satisfactory; this is not one of these assemblies. You must avoid applying glue to the tenon edges, and you should be sparing with the glue so you don't have to deal with squeeze-out.

Begin a simple assembly by gluing one rail to one stile. Apply glue to both ends of the rail but not to the stile. Align the rail carefully before pressing it into the stile. Don't slide the rail back and forth on the stile; that will spread glue into the panel groove, where it shouldn't be. Then fit the finished panel into the panel groove.

After adding the second rail and then the final stile, and after applying some pressure with the clamps, make sure the assembly is square. The fact that cope-and-stick joints aren't self-squaring is just another "gotcha." Measure the diagonals; they should be equal in length. If they aren't equal, loosen the clamps and rack the assembly along the longer diagonal. Reset the clamps and remeasure.

Another assembly "gotcha!" is flatness. Work on a surface you know is flat. Keep the assembly tight against the clamp bars, and don't overtighten the clamps. With a reliable straightedge, check across the stiles, then across the rails, then diagonally. Hunker down and sight across the assembly as you do this to ensure that the assembly isn't visibly twisted.

MULTIPANEL ASSEMBLIES

Framing a single panel is just the beginning. Once you have some experience, you can use frame and panel joinery to make assemblies with multiple panels. Here are some examples: A side for a tall chest might have a horizontal divider — called an intermediate rail — partitioning the frame for two panels. The panels can be identical, or one can be taller than the other. You might have several intermediate rails and several panels.

A wider assembly might have a single vertical divider — called a mullion (or a muntin, a term more appropriate for a divider between glass panes).

Other possibilities include one intermediate rail, one mullion and three panels, or one intermediate rail, two mullions and four panels. An architectural door will typically have a wide lock rail, a couple of intermediate rails and six or eight panels.

When designing the inner frame for a multipanel door, make sure you use the strongest possible arrangement. For assemblies that are taller than they are wide, the intermediate rails should extend unbroken from stile to stile. This arrangement makes it easier to cut and assemble the frame, because all the rails are the same length.

Determining the lengths of the rails and mullions and the dimensions of the panels in one of these complex assemblies follows the same guidelines that govern the simple ones. Rail lengths equal the width of the assembly minus the combined widths of the stiles plus the combined widths of the sticking. (Or, looking at it another way, subtract one sticking width from one stile width. Double that and subtract the amount from the overall assembly width.)

Mullion lengths may be more tricky to determine. If you have just one mullion, extending from top rail to bottom rail, the computation is straightforward. If the vertical space is divided by several rails, you have to lay out the distances from rail to rail. To each of those measurements, add twice the sticking width to determine mullion lengths.

Making the parts is straightforward. Cope the ends of the rails and mullions, then stick the parts. Intermediate rails and mullions are sticked on both edges.

Assembly follows the general guidelines articulated on the previous page, with an extra step. Do a complete dry run. In the course of this, make alignment marks lightly in pencil to help you locate the intermediate rails and the mullions. You can't jam these against the panels as a means of alignment; the panels need expansion clearance.

The practical reason for multipanel constructions is to reduce the size of individual panels. Dividing a frame to create two or more panel spaces is also a great way to modify and improve the appearance of a piece.

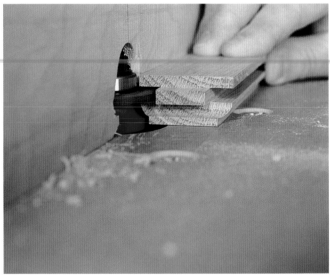

Mullions and intermediate rails that divide a basic frame must be sticked along both edges so they can accommodate panels in both edges.

Begin assembling a multipanel unit by trapping mullions between the rails. A clamp can secure this subassembly as you slide the panels into place. Join the subassembly to one stile.

Next, remove the clamp and fit the large panel — already finished — into place. Add the bottom rail and the second stile.

Apply whatever type of clamps you favor — pipe clamps, bar clamps, or parallel-jaw clamps. Locate one clamp parallel to each rail, with some underneath the assembly and some over the top to even out the clamping pressure. Snug the clamps, and check the assembly for squareness and flatness, just as you would any single-panel assembly.

Multipanel Assemblies

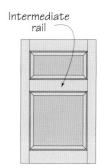

Muntin

Intermediate rail

Two panels

Two panels

Three panels

Three panels

Four panels

APPLIED MOLDINGS

Whereas the decorative profile usually is an integral part of the frame — it's "stuck" there — the molding can be a separate element.

Why a separate molding?

The most obvious reason is so you can use a profile not available using cope-and-stick bits. Sure, you can obtain some additional profiles — such as the quirk-and-bead — by routing them directly on the frame members, but then you have to deal with the tricky business of mitering the sticking.

A special form of separate molding, called a bolection molding, adds depth to the assembly because it stands proud of the frame. Your eye sweeps across the flat frame to the profile, climbs the profile to its peak, then descends to the panel. The only way you can achieve this effect is with a separate moulded strip.

There are other benefits to using separate moldings. One is that you can correct a botched miter without having to completely start over; just cut a new strip of molding. In addition, this construction gives you more options for panels; you can use thicker or thinner material for the panel without having to customize the width of the panel groove. Cut a rabbet, drop the panel into it, then capture it with the molding.

Separate moldings fall into one of two categories: panel moldings or bolection moldings. A panel molding is one that gets glued or bradded to the inside edge of the frame and looks like a stuck molding. It does not project above the face of the frame. Typically, a panel molding is a simple profile, formed in a single pass with a single bit — a bead, ogee or cove-and-bead.

A bolection molding is deeper and has a rabbet cut into its back so it fits over the inner edge — the arris — of the frame. Part of the profile is proud of the frame. A bolection molding generally is a complex profile, combining a full bead and a deep cove, for example, and must be cut in two or more passes using two or more bits.

Routing a Molding

Although a broad array of profile cutting bits are available, every once in a while you may want to produce something custom, something that can't be cut in one pass. Bolection moldings fall into this custom category.

To begin, you must draw the profile you want. Sketch it full size. Using the drawing, select the bits that will cut it, and plan the order in which you'll make the cuts and how you'll support either the router or the workpiece.

Choosing the bit is usually easy enough. For example, coves are formed by cove bits or roundnose bits (often called core box bits).

To work out the workpiece orientation for each cut, hold the bit over the drawing. Ask yourself this: If the bit is in a router table, how must the workpiece approach it for the cut to be placed correctly?

When creating a slender molding, begin with an oversized blank — one that's both wider and longer than the finished molding will be. Make your cuts, then rip it free of the waste.

The following photos show the sequence for cutting the first bolection molding shown in the drawing. It's a cove-and-torus profile, used on the door at right in the photo below.

Bolection moldings are an excellent way of embellishing a flat panel assembly, which otherwise might be rather plain. The molding sets off the border between frame and panel, providing shadow lines and depth. The molding can also provide a means to use contrasting woods as a design feature.

Typical Bolection Moulding Profiles

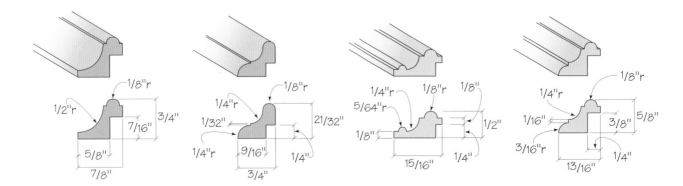

The initial cut on this bolection profile is a ½" cove. To stretch the cove's arc a fraction of an inch, remove the pilot bearing from the bit. The cut is guided by the fence. The blank is the thickness of the molding, but it is wider than the completed molding.

Make the second cut with a bullnose bit, forming the torus shape on the shoulder of the cove. Turn over the blank and make the cut with the top against the tabletop. This bit doesn't have a pilot bearing, so the fence must be aligned with the deepest part of the cutter.

The easiest way to form the rabbet is with a dado cut. When you rip the blank to final size, it will open the dado into a rabbet. The diameter of the bit you use is irrelevant (as long as it's wider than the rabbet must be). Make sure the cut depth is exact.

Rip the molding so the profile falls to the outside of the blade. You'll be able to drive the square-ended waste completely past the blade with your push block. As long as all your blanks were sized consistently to begin, you should end up with uniformly sized moldings.

If for any reason you need to joint the back or bottom of the molding, you can do the job on the router table. Use a jointing fence (it has the outfeed side shimmed a trifle), and position the outfeed side tangent to the cutting edges of the bit. Use carpet tape to stick support strips to the tabletop. The strips can be higher than the rabbet is deep, but they must be narrower than the rabbet is wide. Rest the molding on the strip, the surface to be jointed flat against the fence. Feed the molding across the bit.

Attaching a Separate Molding

There are two ways to mount a panel in a frame with a separate molding. You can cut a rabbet around the inside of the frame to create a ledge for the panel. With the panel resting on the rabbet, glue and perhaps brad the molding in place to secure the panel.

The other approach is to attach the decorative molding to the frame, again using glue and perhaps brads. Then insert the panel from the back and secure it with a retainer strip.

I prefer the latter approach because it allows for securely gluing the molding and cleaning up any squeeze-out. Without the panel, you easily can apply clamps to hold the molding while the glue sets. There's no risk that hidden, inaccessible squeeze-out will fasten a panel, which usually needs freedom to expand and contract, to the frame.

When you do install the panel, you can brad the retainer to the frame rather than glue it. Exposed fasteners on the inside of the door are seldom an aesthetic drawback.

Installing the panel as a separate operation allows you to apply a finish to the panel and to the frame and molding individually.

Capturing Panels with Separate Mouldings

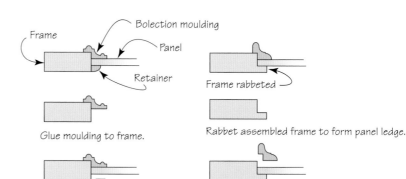

Glue moulding to frame.

Set panel against moulding, secure with retainer. Size the retainer to come flush with the face of the frame.

Rabbet assembled frame to form panel ledge.

Set panel on ledge and secure with moulding. Trim moulding or rabbet to ensure a tight fit of the moulding to the frame and to the panel.

Cutting moldings to fit the frames need not be entirely trial and error. Miter one end of each strip and tuck that end into the frame. Measure from the frame member to the heel of the miter. At the other end, measure and mark the same dimension on the molding. That's the heel of the cut.

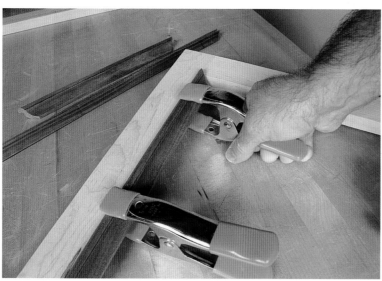

If the molding is applied before the panel is installed, the width of the frame is no impediment to clamping. You can locate the clamps on the inside rather than having to span the width of the rail or stile to reach the molding.

Use "go-sticks" to clamp retainer strips against the frame. A go-stick is a thin scrap of straight-grained stock crosscut slightly longer than the span from retainer to retainer. Flex the go-stick enough to fit it between the retainers, then relax your hold and allow it to jam against the retainers, holding them while the glue sets.

Routing a rabbet is a simple operation, but here the cut is substantial — typically $1/2$" to $5/8$" deep and $3/8$" wide. I use an extended base plate to keep the router steady, and I block up the frame so the rabbet bit's pilot doesn't dig into the bench top as full depth is reached. In some instances, climb-cutting is appropriate — and safe — to minimize chipping at the margins of the cut. Once the rabbet is cut, the inside corners must be squared with a chisel (inset). Perfection isn't necessary, because the molding will conceal your handwork.

Where the frame is rabbeted, the molding captures the panel. As always, apply finish to the panel before assembly, and cut the molding pieces to fit prior to opening the glue container. When you assemble the unit, elevate the frame so you can get clamps around it. Protect the molding itself; use rippings that have a cove or V-groove cut from end to end as cauls.

[CHAPTER *three*]

making panels

Right off the bat, recognize that you have a wealth of panel options. Raised panels may be your primary focus, but they don't have to be. You can make your assemblies with flat, solid-wood panels, with veneered panels, or with plywood panels. They can be plain, overlaid or shouldered as well as raised.

Because raised panels probably are your reason for reading this, let's get to them. Unless you have a shaper, the router is the best tool in your shop for raising panels.

Some people use the table saw or radial-arm saw to raise panels in a straight bevel, but there are some distinct shortcomings to this method. First, you can get only a straight bevel. In addition, the saw blade will probably leave fairly prominent marks that will take a lot of sanding to eradicate. Finally, you can't produce the tongue around the panel that fits so nicely into the groove in the frame.

Like panel-raising shaper cutters, all panel-raising router bits are designed to form a tongue — dimensioned to match a sticking cutter's groove — around the panel. Panel-raising tools produce a far smoother cut than a saw blade. You'll have to sand the cut, sure, but not nearly as much as you would a sawed panel. Finally, you have a pretty interesting assortment of profiles from which to choose.

For many, raised panels are what it's all about. These panels were raised using a variety of techniques and cutters, and it's all explained in the pages that follow.

Veneering allows you to embellish a project with flamboyant burls and other figured patterns without breaking the budget. You glue thin slices of these exotics to flat, stable materials like MDF or plywood and clamp them in a shop-made press constructed of melamine and stout cauls.

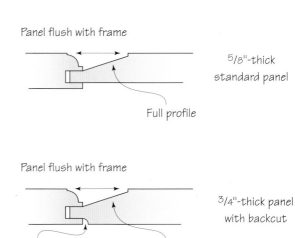

Panel flush with frame

5/8"-thick standard panel

Full profile

Panel flush with frame

3/4"-thick panel with backcut

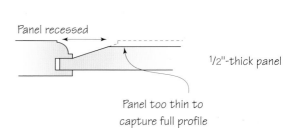

Backcut   Full profile

Panel recessed

1/2"-thick panel

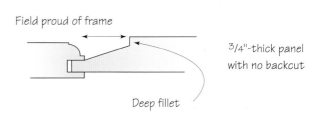

Panel too thin to capture full profile

Field proud of frame

3/4"-thick panel with no backcut

Deep fillet

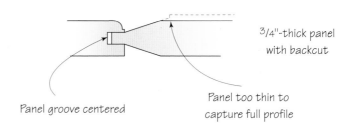

3/4"-thick panel with backcut

Panel groove centered

Panel too thin to capture full profile

Raised Panels

FLAT PANELS

The term *flat panel* suggests something bland or utilitarian — a door with a birch plywood panel, for example. But many other flat panel designs and styles belie that characterization of blandness. Certainly, the flat panel assembly typically is a low-key one. But as the Shakers demonstrated with their cabinetry, low-key design is often extremely elegant.

Plywood

Use hardwood plywood or hardwood-veneered MDF for the panel. Both are available in a wide array of species — maple, cherry, the oaks, walnut, mahogany and many others — even in the $\frac{1}{4}$" thickness. You won't find much at the "Big Box" home center, but many plywood wholesalers will sell you a sheet or two on a cash-and-carry basis.

The advantages are several:
- The appearance is good.
- Work is reduced: no boards to cut, joint, plane, glue up, and sand. Just cut the panels to size from the 4' × 8' sheet.
- Sheet goods like plywood and MDF are stable. The panel won't expand and contract, so you can glue it into the frame, thus reinforcing the entire assembly. It won't warp and twist the door you are constructing.

Given a choice, I'd take a hardwood-veneered MDF over a comparable sheet of plywood. MDF stays flat, and its thickness is more accurate than that of plywood.

Beyond these manufactured goods, you can veneer $\frac{1}{4}$" plywood or MDF with purchased or shop-sawn veneers. This choice can be an economical way to get spectacular grain into your project. As we'll see at the end of the chapter, you can bookmatch veneers in a panel, or bookmatch pairs of panels. You can create geometric patterns by applying four leaves in butt, diamond and reverse-diamond matches.

The primary difficulty in any of these approaches may be in matching the panel to the standard panel groove. Plywood is notoriously undersized, so a nominal $\frac{1}{4}$" thickness will rattle in a standard panel groove. Veneer the panel, and it will be thicker than the groove is wide.

You can resolve the first problem by using a metric or a plywood cutter to cut the groove. Amana Tool sells cope-and-stick bit sets in several profiles, especially for this application; the tools, called In-Stile, can be adjusted to vary the width of the groove.

Where the panel is thicker than $\frac{1}{4}$" and the frame stock too thin to accommodate a wider groove, you can back-cut the panel. Because the panel is stable, you can cut a rabbet that tightly abuts the rails and stiles, thus concealing the multi-ply edges.

For a utilitarian cabinet, relatively inexpensive plywood is suitable for a panel. This door has a birch frame housing a $\frac{1}{4}$"-thick birch plywood panel.

Using hardwood plywood for panels saves you time. In the time it takes to crosscut rough stock into panel-size pieces ready for surfacing, you can break down a plywood sheet into panel-size pieces ready for installation.

Solid Wood

The choice of solid wood for a panel doesn't mean that the panel must be raised. The Shakers didn't have manufactured sheets from which to saw panels, and they favored the flat panel. They used solid wood and backcut (or undercut; choose your terminology) the edges to fit the panel to the panel groove.

This choice means you have to deal with all the stock prep tasks: selecting the wood, planing it to thickness, jointing the edges for gluing up wider panels, and so on. After you've sized the panel, you can perform the panel-raising operation itself.

A flat veneered panel is just a little out of the ordinary, and veneering isn't difficult or expensive. It doesn't require unusual tools, either. You glue veneer to both sides of a stable material like MDF or plywood. Fitting the panel to a standard panel groove may require you to rabbet the back (inset).

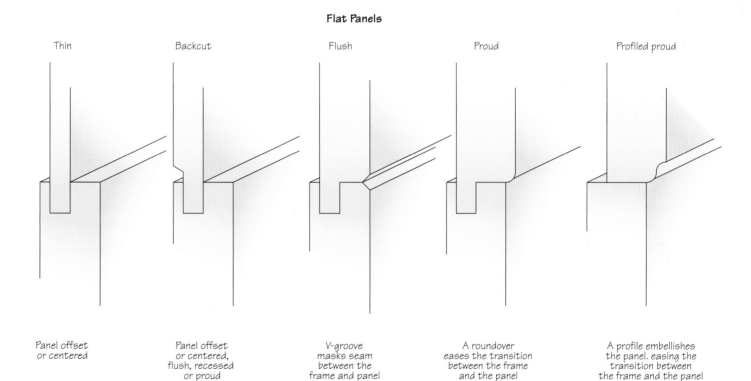

Flat Panels

Thin	Backcut	Flush	Proud	Profiled proud
Panel offset or centered	Panel offset or centered, flush, recessed or proud	V-groove masks seam between the frame and panel	A roundover eases the transition between the frame and the panel	A profile embellishes the panel. easing the transition between the frame and the panel

PREPARING STOCK FOR RAISED PANELS

The first step here is to select a panel thickness. The industry convention is to use $\frac{5}{8}$"-thick stock for the panels. This thickness, in conjunction with a standard $\frac{3}{4}$"-thick frame constructed with standard cope-and-stick cutters, will yield an assembly that's just right for running through a wide-belt sander. The raised field of the panel will be flush with the faces of the rails and stiles. When you shape the panel, you work only the face of the panel, not the back or the edges.

That's the industry standard.

If you want a panel that deviates, that's a bit nonstandard, you may have to use something other than $\frac{5}{8}$"-thick stock. In fact, an awful lot of wood-workers do use $\frac{3}{4}$"-thick stock for raised panels even though they want the standard look.

To achieve that look with $\frac{3}{4}$" stock, you simply have to "undercut" the back of the panel. The undercut — a sort of rabbet — produces a relief in the back of the panel so the tongue is $\frac{1}{4}$" thick. Undercutting can be done with a rab-beting bit or a slotting cutter; dedicated undercutters are also available.

Looking at it one way, using an un-dercutter separates the process of fit-ting the panel to the groove from that of establishing the optimum appear-ance. You have to deal with only one issue at a time. If you want the panel's raised field to be proud of the frame — to be a so-called projecting panel — you can do that pretty easily. Cutting the profile deeper won't compromise the fit to the groove.

From a different vantage point, the undercutter represents yet another bit and another setup and another cut (and another opportunity for a goof).

To make undercutters easier to deal with, most bit makers have mounted them right on the raiser. You don't have an additional bit and setup to struggle with. You set up the bit once

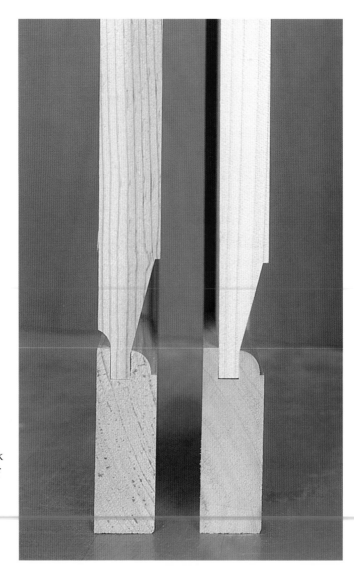

These assemblies look the same from the front, but the panel on the left is made from $\frac{3}{4}$"-thick stock and is under-cut. The right panel is $\frac{5}{8}$"-thick, so un-dercutting was not necessary to fit it to the standard panel groove.

and machine both the panel face and back simultaneously. One benefit is that you always get a perfect tongue, regardless of the face relief, but you can run through a lot of test stock as you creep up on the right bit elevation.

An operational limitation of the bit configuration is that fence positioning is your only means of moderating the volume of material removed in a pass. You can't make a pass with the bit set low then raise it for a second pass, as you can with a backcutter-free bit. This shouldn't be a problem, but it is a limi-tation you should be aware of.

This "two cuts in one" feature is available only in the horizontal form of panel-raising tools. On a vertical panel-raising tool, the cutting axis is rotated 90°, and it isn't possible to out-

fit the bit with a backcutter. You can, of course, use a separate backcutter.

Having sorted through the options and picked one, plane the stock to the thickness you've chosen. If necessary, glue up the wood to produce the widths needed, and crosscut the rough panels to finished length.

Remember that the straightness and flatness of the panel is as important to the overall straightness and flatness of the structure as the frame is. In most circumstances, if the panel is warped, it will twist the frame. So choose the panel stock accordingly. Of course, some of the prettiest wood is also the most gnarly and unstable. The trick is to keep this stock thin enough that it can't overpower the frame and warp it.

Sizing the Panels

Before you can raise the panels, you have to rip and crosscut them to size. In establishing the panel dimensions, you have to account for the relative moisture content of the wood. The length of the panel won't change over time, but the width will come and go with the seasons.

You should have an easy slip fit during assembly. If the panel material (and the frame stock, too) were perfectly stable, you could measure from the bottom of one groove to the bottom of the opposite one and cut the panel to that dimension minus about $1/16$" for assembly clearance. But, of course, no solid-wood stock is really stable. Because wood doesn't get longer when it expands, you need to allow only that $1/16$" assembly clearance in the length.

Ripping the panel to width is a little trickier. In the dead of a cold winter, when the relative humidity is generally low and the furnace's heat dries the shop air even more, stock is as shrunken as it will ever be. The cabinetmaker's rule of thumb is to allow for expansion about $1/8$" per 1' of width. Don't forget the assembly clearance. At this time of year, cut panels underwidth so they'll have room to expand as summer approaches.

In the slough of a sultry summer, on the other hand, stock is as swollen with moisture as it will get. Cut it to fit pretty tightly in the frame; make it about $1/16$" less than the groove-to-groove dimension.

One final advisory: Be open to dividing a really wide panel. Add a frame mullion extending from rail to rail midway between the stiles, and use two panels instead of one. This is a bit of extra work, but it will ensure you don't see daylight between the panel's edge and the stile in the dry season. It probably will improve the appearance of the assembly.

Stock selection is critical to the appearance of solid-wood panels. The ideal is to always make panels of individual wide boards, like the 13"-wide spalted maple board (top right) that yielded the panel at left. But even narrow boards like the sassafras ones at left, if matched with care according to color and figure, can be glued up to produce attractive panels (right). You ought to avoid the sort of mismatching evident in the panel at bottom front.

PANEL-RAISING BITS

The first issue you have to deal with in raising panels on the router table is the bit. You have two basic configurations from which to choose. The optimum setups are different, depending on the bit.

A panel-raising bit is as big a router bit as you will buy and represents as big a cut as the router can make. It's both serious business and a big investment.

Two configurations are available: horizontal and vertical.

Horizontal Panel-Raising Bits

If you are used to standard straight, roundover and cove bits, the typical horizontal panel-raising bit will look huge. The (orange) horizontal panel-raising bit shown at right is just under $3\frac{1}{2}$" in diameter and weighs 11 ounces. That's a lot of metal to spin.

The size of these bits is their drawback, of course. You need a high-horsepower router with variable speed to run them safely and effectively.

Fifteen years ago, such bits looked like two-bladed airplane propellers. Nowadays, chip-limiting designs have become commonplace. By restricting the size of the chip, the cutting edge can remove, the designs reduce the chance for kickback. In addition, you may see three-wing bits, as well as some with extra, small, shear-cutting tips. These extra cutting edges help smooth the cut.

The reason these bits are so big, of course, is the demand for a wide reveal. If you want a 1"-wide reveal plus a $\frac{3}{8}$"-wide tongue for the panel groove — this is pretty standard in the cabinet industry, where shapers are used to raise panels — you need a bit that's just about $3\frac{1}{2}$" in diameter. A smaller bit will suffice if you are willing to accept a narrower reveal — $\frac{7}{8}$", for example, or $\frac{3}{4}$" or even $\frac{1}{2}$".

Most manufacturers carry three to six profiles in their catalogs, though a few manufacturers have extravagant assortments. The point: Don't feel limited to a beveled reveal; you can have an ogee, a cove or any of these shapes with a bead around the panel's field.

The horizontal configuration is the most common for panel-raising bits. Though the large, $3\frac{1}{2}$" bits dominate, smaller bits that produce narrower bevels are available. A narrow bevel will give an out-of-the-ordinary appearance to your project, and the smaller bit will be easier and safer to use.

Vertical panel-raising bits are generally smaller in diameter than their horizontal counterparts. They can be run at full speed in any midsize, table-mounted router. Because they lack pilot bearings, you can't use these bits for curved-edge panels.

Vertical Panel-Raising Bits

Although still pretty massive, a vertical panel-raising bit is small in comparison to an equivalent horizontal one. It is much taller than a horizontal bit, but it's no more than 1½" in diameter and often even less. That reduced diameter is the whole point. Driven at 22,000 rpm, the tip speed of the vertical bit is just under 100 mph (compared to 230 mph for the horizontal bit).

The design concept is simple: Change the angle of attack. The reveal is dictated by the bit height rather than its diameter. Vertical panel-raising bits currently on the market will cut a standard 1" reveal plus tongue (but nothing less). Available patterns include ogees, coves and standard bevels.

One trade-off is that the quality of the cut is somewhat diminished over that of a horizontal bit. The vertical bit does have a greater tendency to leave mill marks. All this means is that you have to sand a bit longer.

The typical vertical bit has two flutes. Because it has no pilot, it has to be used in conjunction with a fence; therefore, it cannot be used to raise the edges of curved panels.

Undercutters

A subset of the horizontal panel-raising bits are those with undercutters.

The undercutter produces a rabbet-like recess on the back of the panel. This allows you to use ¾"-thick stock for panels without having to cut excessively deep with the panel-raising bit. An undercut panel ends up being flush with both the face and the back of a standard frame.

An undercutter can be purchased as a separate bit. After raising the panels, use the undercutter to relieve that panel back as necessary to size the tongue.

The undercutter is often mated with a horizontal panel-raising bit; both cutters are on the same shank. You can argue that the configuration, which

places the work between two cutters, is hazardous, but you shouldn't have problems if you use well-placed hold-downs. It's worth noting that with this bit, you creep up on the final cut depth not by adjusting the bit height but by shifting the fence position. (An alternative would be to remove the undercutter for the first two or three passes. Reinstall it for the final pass only.)

Horizontal raisers with backcutters (left) are popular because they produce a tongue of a predictable thickness (¼") on stock ⅝" and thicker. They typically are used with ¾"-thick stock because that reduces stock prep. Though most such bits do have pilot bearings, the one shown does not. It can't be used to produce curved-edge panels. The bit (right) for Shaker-style doors cuts a rabbet with a beveled, rather than square, shoulder. I consider it a type of backcutter because the Shakers oriented the cut to the inside.

Common Raised-Panel Profiles

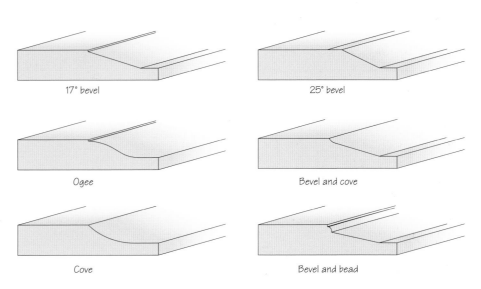

17° bevel

25° bevel

Ogee

Bevel and cove

Cove

Bevel and bead

USING A HORIZONTAL BIT

If you plan to use a horizontal bit, before you do anything else, make sure your router will accommodate it. As I've said before, you need high horsepower and speed control for a horizontal bit. In addition, your router's structure must accept it. The opening in the mounting plate or tabletop has to be large enough to accept a $3\frac{1}{2}$"-diameter bit, of course, but check the router, too.

Most big plunge routers have tabs that project into the base's bit opening (template guides screw to these tabs). A big panel-raising bit will hit these tabs. This doesn't mean you can't use these routers for the job. However, it does mean that the mounting plate's thickness is a big part of your margin of bit-height adjustment. Even with the bit set as low as you can get it, its cutting edges may be fully exposed above the table surface. To make a "shallow" cut, you may have to set the fence overcenter on the bit, and you'll address less than the full reveal width. (You reduce the width of the cut rather than the depth of it.) For the second and subsequent passes, you move the fence back.

The secondary hassle caused by these tabs is that of installing the bit in the collet. To get the shank in the collet, you'll have to have the motor bottomed against the base, allowing you precious little room to work the wrench or wrenches on the collet nut.

With the bit in the router, set it to an approximate height. The goal is to set the bit for the final cut, but you establish exactly what that is through test cuts on stock of the correct thickness. You need to set the fence before you can do that.

Don't forget to dial back the router speed. Set the router to run as slow as possible.

The horizontal bit is the home-shop standard for producing raised panels. It's an expeditious, flexible way to do the work, and the results are excellent.

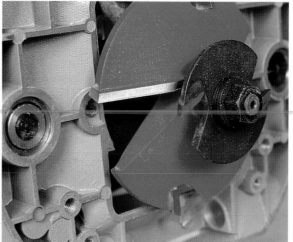

Not every router will accommodate a full-size horizontal panel-raising bit. This plunge router's base doesn't have an opening large enough for the bit. You can still use the bit in the router, but you have to be careful to avoid contact between the bit and the base. If this is the sort of router you have, you may do better with a smaller-diameter bit or with a vertical bit.

This plunge router has an opening in the base designed to accommodate the largest-diameter bits available. It's easy to install the bit, and you have a greater range for height adjustment.

Setting the Fence and Hold Downs

Even if the bit has a pilot, use a fence to guide and help you control straight cuts. The fence gives you much better control of the work than does the bit's pilot alone.

The standard setup rules apply here. Tailor the bit opening, if at all possible, to conform to the bit contour. Position the fence tangent to the pilot bearing, but make sure the pilot is just out of contact with the work.

Use a fence with an upright face (as opposed to a plain flat board); this provides a place to clamp holddowns like featherboards. A basic, one-board fence will guide the workpiece, but you ought to use featherboards to control it and prevent it from lifting from the tabletop. Use a fence with a 3"- or 4"-high back, and clamp a couple of featherboards to it, one on either side of the bit.

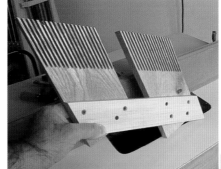

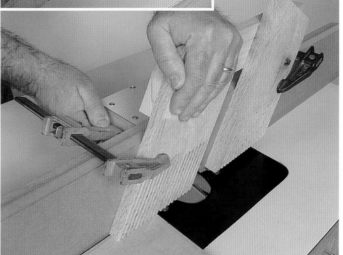

Shop-made wooden featherboards are my preference. I think they have better traction, which makes them better at resisting kickback. This tandem setup — just two featherboards screwed to a cleat — mounts to the fence with just two clamps and places one featherboard on either side of the bit.

A horizontal bit can be set by measurement if you have a device to gauge the elevation of the cutting edges adjacent to the bearing. Those form the panel's tongue, which must be $1/4$" thick. If you are raising a $5/8$"-thick panel, those edges must be $3/8$" above the table. My shop-made setup gauge straddles the cutter, allowing me to measure the elevation.

It's best to use the fence to guide the cut whenever possible. You must position it tangent to the pilot bearing to get the cutter's full profile. Hold a straightedge against the fence as you swing it into position. My ideal is to position the fence just clear of the bearing. Watch the bearing as you slide the straightedge. The straightedge should graze the bearing without turning it.

TEST-CUTS

To confirm your setup, make a test-cut (or two or more). You need to be sure, before you raise the actual panels, that the appearance is what you want and that the tongue will fit the groove. This final setup is the starting point for your cuts, regardless of how you approach the operation.

I prefer to raise panels in stages, making a shallow cut that removes about half the waste, followed by a second and final pass. The best way to manage this is by shifting the fence position.

With the typical horizontal bit (even one with an integral backcutter), you really only adjust the bit elevation at this test-cut stage. You have set the fence in relation to the pilot bearing. Presuming that you want to raise the panels with progressive cuts, you can shift the fence forward for that light first pass, then reset it tangent to the pilot bearing. This move won't impact the featherboards. They'll ride along with the fence and apply the same downward pressure regardless of where on the tabletop you position the fence.

For your final test-cut, shift the fence and make a first pass on a sample of the working stock. Reset the fence against the bearing and make your second pass. Check the sample for appearance and for its fit in the frame's panel groove. If necessary, raise or lower the bit and make another round of test-cuts.

When you have the setting nailed, recheck your featherboards. Take up your good stock, and raise some panels.

The proof of your setup is in the fit of the panel to its groove in the frame. Make a test-cut on a sample of the panel stock, and fit it to an actual frame member. If the panel drops into the groove, reduce the cut depth a hair. If it's a force fit, increase the cut depth a hair. The ideal is snug fitting.

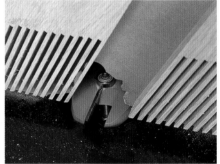

Staging the cuts — beginning with a shallow initial cut and producing the full profile in progressively deeper cuts — isn't absolutely necessary, but it is advisable. I do it by clamping a reference block against the back edge of the fence to capture the final position. Then, for the initial cut, I swing one end of the fence forward and away from the block (top left) so only the outer tips of the bit extend beyond the fence (top right). The featherboards move with the fence, of course. You can feed the workpiece by hand or with a push block (above).

MAKING THE CUTS

Cut across the end grain first. This cut is most likely to cause tear-out, but any tear-out will almost surely be routed away when you make the long-grain cuts. Work your way around the panel: end grain, long grain, second end grain, second long grain and done.

Make your first, shallow cut on every workpiece, then adjust the setup to increase the cut. Depending on how you've set up things, this adjustment may involve moving the fence or mere-ly raising the bit. Make a second pass on every piece, adjust the setup, and so forth.

When you are finished, you probably will need to sand the cuts lightly. Especially when cutting across the grain, the bit tends to lay the end grain down a little. The wood will feel smooth to the touch when you stroke in one direction but rough when you stroke in the other direction. A couple of light passes with a pad sander should take care of this.

The final pass is made with the fence tight against the reference block (far left) so the fence is tangent to the pilot bearing (left). The workpiece handling is the same on each cut in the progression.

USING A VERTICAL BIT

Setup is a little more complicated for a vertical bit. Because it doesn't have a pilot bearing, you have to find both the optimum bit elevation and the optimum fence setting via test-cuts. Fortunately, you can creep up on both.

For now, you have the bit in the router and you've made a coarse bit-height setting. Deal with the fence next.

The cut itself doesn't reveal that a vertical bit produced it. The lesson is that you need only a modest setup to produce attractive raised panels.

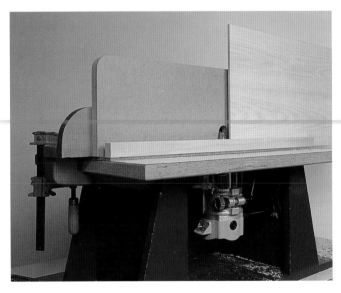

The vertical panel-raising bit is a perfect match for smaller router tables, especially those with midpower routers. An older, 1½-hp router in my benchtop router table has what it takes to raise panels, so long as a vertical bit does the actual cutting.

The trap fence I use with a vertical panel-raising bit has a tall facing that fits against the regular fence. To attach the accessory fence, loosen the regular fence's clamps enough to slide the base under the regular fence, then fasten the trap facing to the regular fence with screws or, as I do, with studded plastic knobs (one is on the regular fence's base).

Fence Configuration

A tall fence, often a unit made especially for the job, is a common complement to a vertical bit. The rationale is that a tall fence will more readily support a panel that's 24" or more in height. Make a fence with a broad base, a 12"-high face and lots of brackets bracing the vertical face. With this fence, use a featherboard set to hold the panel tight to the fence through the cut.

My preference is to use a trap fence. This is a strip of wood clamped to the table parallel to the fence. It creates a channel for the workpiece to move through, preventing its bottom edge from skidding away from the fence. The trap fence works great in conjunction with a commonplace fence, one with a face that's 3" or 4" high. Apply modest pressure to the workpiece just above the fence, to lever it against the trap fence.

The hassle of the trap fence is the setup. (You have the same hassle with a featherboard, by the way.) Whenever you move the main fence, you have to move the trap fence. The typical cutting sequence dictates that you move the fence at least once.

My solution is an add-on facing and trap fence for my standard fence. The facing is a piece of ³/₄"-thick MDF, drilled and threaded for four studded knobs. The knobs mount the MDF to the regular fence. Screwed to the bottom of the facing is a piece of hardboard with the trap fence attached to it. I use a strip of the panel stock as a gauge between the trap fence and the facing when fastening the hardboard to the facing. The hardboard extends under the fence, so when I clamp it to the tabletop, it provides additional security for the trap fence. Thereafter, moving the fence also moves the trap fence.

Be forewarned that the setup does have a pitfall. It's easy to gouge the cut on the second or third pass if you apply any feed pressure in line with the cut itself. The cut won't be supported by the fence after the first pass. The solution is a well-placed featherboard. Perch it on a block to get above the cut, and clamp it to the tabletop. It should press the workpiece against the facing just above the bit.

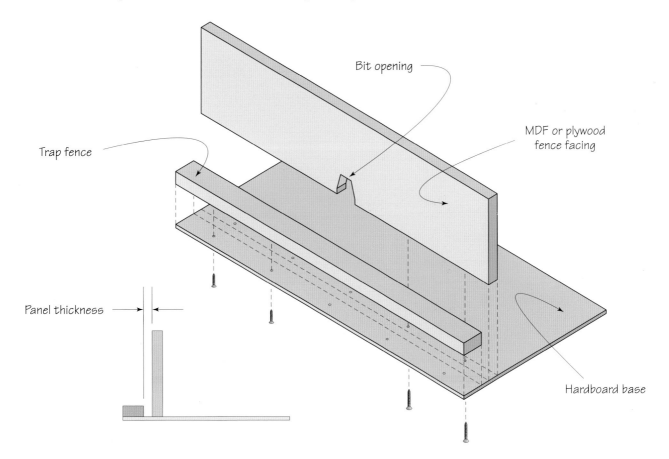

Trap fence

Bit opening

MDF or plywood fence facing

Panel thickness

Hardboard base

Trap Fence

Dialing In the Setup

With the fence itself assembled but tem-
porarily moved back from the tabletop
bit opening, adjust the vertical bit. Set
the bit elevation by eye (or against a
ruler). The bit's vertical exposure equals
the width of the cut on the panel.

Now shift the fence into position.
Measure from the cutting edge to the
trap fence edge to establish a prelimi-
nary position. With $\frac{5}{8}$"-thick stock, the
tongue needs to be $\frac{1}{4}$" thick, so the gap
between the trap fence and the cutting
edge needs to be $\frac{1}{4}$".

What I do at this stage is capture
this rough fence setting by tucking
scraps against the back edge of the
fence on each side and clamping them
to the table. That allows me to shift the
fence forward a little to make a light
cut on a test piece and then return it to
the previous position for the full cut.

The blocks also provide a baseline
for further adjustments. If my test-cut
reveals I'm cutting a little too deep
(meaning the tongue is too thin and
rattles in the panel groove), I can pull
the fence away from one or both
blocks, either using a shim or simply
by measuring. (If you are smitten with
dial indicator precision, you can use
feeler gauges or the dial indicator to
measure fence movement from this
baseline.) If the cut is too shallow,
bump the blocks away from the fence
using shims or your ruler measurement, reclamp them, and then move
the fence back against them.

This approach works with the kind
of low-rent fence I prefer, as well as the
most super-duper commercial fence.
The adjustment will be as precise as
the measuring device you use (eyeball
and ruler, feeler gauge, dial indicator).

To get the exact setting you want
with these pilot-free bits, get the reveal
width nailed, then work on the reveal
depth. That means you refine the bit
height first, then the fence position.
Make each test-cut in two passes by
shifting the fence.

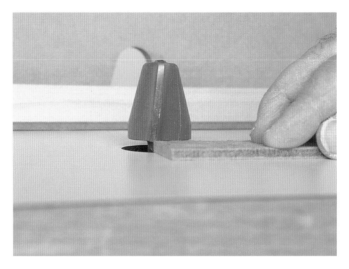

The bit must be fully elevated to produce the entire profile, including the tongue. The trap fence has a base, so you must elevate
the bit above that. Use a scrap of the base material — here $\frac{1}{4}$"-
thick hardboard — as a gauge beside the bit. My fence is separate
from the table, and I can drop it over the bit after the bit height is
set. If you can't do this, you'll have to sight through the panel
channel to the bit to set its height.

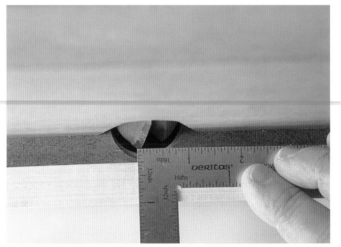

Set the fence with
a rule, measuring
between the trap
fence and the cut-
ting edges of the
fat part of the bit.
The tongue should
be $\frac{1}{4}$" thick, so the
gap should be that
wide.

Make a test-cut to
confirm the bit
height and fence
position are proper-
ly set for the final fit
you want. The test
stock needs to be
the same thickness
as the panels, but it
doesn't need to be
very long or wide.
Check the tongue's
fit in a piece of the
sticked frame.

Making the Cuts

Once your test-cuts prove you have the bit set to the right height and the fence positioned correctly, cut the panels. Pull the fence forward, away from the stop blocks, for the first pass. For the first pass, I forego the featherboard. After a first cut is made along each edge of each panel, I set the fence back against the blocks, then set the featherboard. Then I make the final pass.

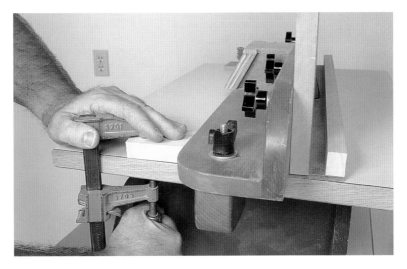

Assuming the test-cut confirms your setup, butt a reference block against the back edge of the fence and clamp it to the tabletop. Then you can back the fence away from it to stage the panel-raising cuts. If your fence doesn't permit you to move just one end, clamp blocks against both ends.

On the initial pass especially, you can rely on the trap fence alone to control the panel as you cut. Keep your hand pressure high on the panel, forcing the top against the tall fence and thereby levering the bottom edge against the trap fence. This method may take some conscious effort to do; it does for me because my instinct is to put the pressure low on the fence.

Before the final pass, when the fence is back against the stops, take a moment to set up a featherboard. To ensure the featherboard's pressure is above the cut, set it on a block, as shown above. This will help you maintain uniform pressure throughout each cut on the panel's four edges.

RAISING PANELS WITHOUT A PANEL-RAISING BIT

A mortising bit and a little ingenuity allow you to raise panels with a straight bevel. No panel-raising bit is required.

You'll need only a router table, a router — even a 1-hp model will do — and a shop-made jig. The bit required is intended for routing hinge mortises, but I use this type of bit regularly for cutting tenons, laps and even rabbets. The bits are available in sizes up to $1\frac{1}{2}$" in diameter, with and without a shank-mounted bearing. (You don't need the bearing here.)

The jig design, created by Pennsylvania cabinetmaker Glenn Bostock, appeals to me because the jig allows some degree of control over the width and angle of the bevel. Panel-raising bits, both horizontal and vertical, are highly standardized. The popular $3\frac{1}{2}$"-diameter horizontal bits cut a $\frac{3}{8}$"-wide tongue and a 1"-wide bevel.

The particular jig shown in the photo raises a $1\frac{1}{4}$"-wide bevel on a $\frac{5}{8}$"-thick panel with a tongue that is $\frac{1}{4}$" thick and $\frac{3}{8}$" wide. The fillet between the bevel and the raised field will be $\frac{3}{32}$" high. It is easy to make a jig to accommodate a larger or smaller bit (or even a dish cutter, which would give you a cove between the bevel and the field). I have both smaller and larger mortising bits, so I can rout narrower bevels or wider ones.

Three parts make up the jig: a base, a rabbeted fence and a runner. Dimensions are shown in the drawing. The fence and the runner are attached, parallel to each other to the base, shown on the next page. They are scaled and positioned to present the panel to the bit at just the correct angle for the bevel cut. A hole for the bit in the base is tangent to the fence. (If your router table's bit opening is centered, you will have to alter the jig dimensions so you can position it properly and still secure it with clamps.)

To make your own jig, cut the parts to size, rabbet the fence and drill the bit hole in the base. Assemble the parts with screws driven through the base into the fence and runner.

Using the Jig

Rip and crosscut the panels to size.

Because of the angle at which the bit addresses the panel, the fillet around the raised field will be slightly undercut. You can square it with a shoulder plane after the panel is raised, or you can saw a shallow kerf to define the raised field right at the outset. I do the latter.

Rabbet all four edges of each panel. A $\frac{3}{8}$"-wide and -deep rabbet will transform into a $\frac{1}{4}$"-thick by $\frac{3}{8}$"-long tongue on a $\frac{5}{8}$"-thick panel. Use the mortising bit in concert with the table's fence to cut the rabbet.

The jig is simple: two strips of wood, one of them rabbeted, attached to a thin plywood base. The jig is used on the router table with a mortising bit, available in several diameters from several manufacturers. With it, you produce straight-bevel raised panels like the two resting on the jig.

Now set the jig on the table, and position the hole in the base over the bit. Align the jig so the bit's cutting edges are tangent to the rabbeted fence. Set the bit using a rabbeted length of the panel stock. Lay the work across the runner and lower its rabbeted edge into the fence's rabbet. Sight across the tabletop to the bit with the panel just behind it. Adjust the bit height and the fence position so the tips of the cutting edges just align with the place where the shoulder and base of the panel's rabbet meet. Clamp the jig to the tabletop.

To rout the bevels, set the piece on the runner and fence and feed it across the bit. Start with a cross-grained cut so that, as you work around the panel, you'll end with a long-grain cut. Hold the panel firmly against the bottom of the fence rabbet and down on the runner.

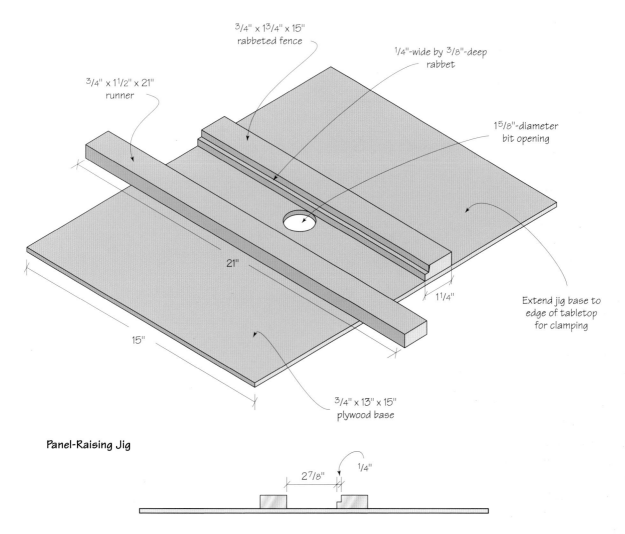

3/4" x 1³/4" x 15"
rabbeted fence

¹/4"-wide by ³/8"-deep
rabbet

3/4" x 1¹/2" x 21"
runner

1⁵/8"-diameter
bit opening

21"

1¹/4"

15"

Extend jig base to
edge of tabletop
for clamping

3/4" x 13" x 15"
plywood base

Panel-Raising Jig

2⁷/8"   ¹/4"

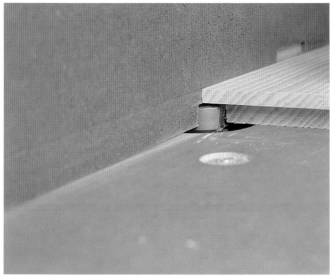

To form the panel's tongue, rout a rabbet around the blank's edge. I usually install the mortising bit I'm going to use to cut the bevels in the table-mounted router, then I use it with the fence to produce the rabbets. The rabbet should be no more than ³/8" wide and should leave a ¹/4"-thick tongue.

The tongue has to fit the panel grooves that have already been cut. A good fit is essential; rather than just measuring, check the fit in an actual frame member.

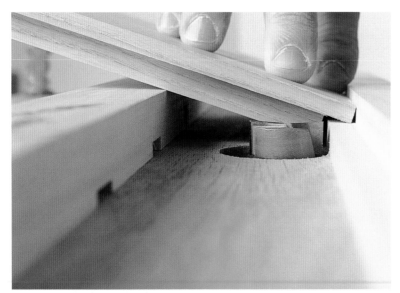

To set the height of the bit, hunker down and sight through the jig's feed channel to the bit. Hold a rabbeted panel blank on the fence and runner, right up against the bit. You'll see how much material the bit must clear. Don't set the bit to hog away the bevel in one pass. Stage the cut.

Rest the panel on the fence and runner, and feed it across the bit. Stand so the rabbeted fence is at your left hand and the runner is at your right. Push the panel away from you across the cutter. (Feeding from the other end is climb-cutting, which is inadvisable.) Use a push block, of course; the shop-made one shown at left has a heel to catch the edge of the panel. If you make too heavy a cut, the panel may ride up on the bit and twist to your right. (I repeat, stage the cut.) A divot in the tongue (inset) is the result. It won't show in the final assembly.

Designing a Jig

To make a jig to accommodate a different bit size or panel thickness, sketch a full-scale layout on paper, following the steps in the illustration below.

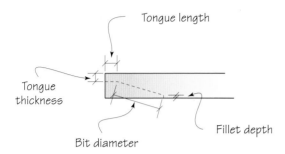

1. Lay out the desired panel profile.

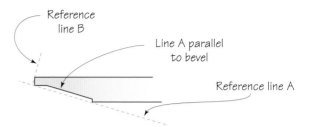

2. Draw reference line A from the corner of the tongue and parallel to the bevel. The draw the reference line B from the panel's back corner perpendicular to A.

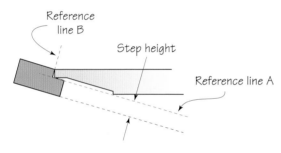

3. Sketch the rabbeted fence. Step height equals the depth of the rabbet necessary to produce the tongue on the panel.

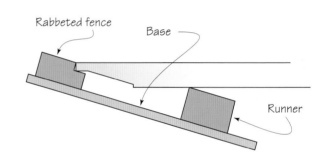

4. Sketch a runner wherever the gap between the base and the panel matches the runner's thickness.

Jig Design

RAISING PANELS ON A TABLE SAW

The table saw is an ideal machine for raising straight-bevel panels. It is particularly good if your project doesn't fit within the boundaries the router sets up.

Those boundaries include limits on the width and angle of the straight bevels that the router bit cuts. Working on the table saw, you can bevel one or both faces of a panel. You also can cut a narrow bevel or a wide one.

In terms of cutting power, the saw doesn't require multiple passes to complete a bevel. But you do have to make shoulder cuts, then bevel cuts, and it is likely that sanding of the sawn surface will be necessary.

Here's how to raise a straight-bevel panel that has a fillet or shoulder between the bevel and the field:

• The fillet is usually about $1/16$" high, so set the blade only that high. Set the rip fence to the width of the bevel by measuring from the fence to the outside of the blade. Kerf the panel parallel to all four edges.

• Now set up the saw for the bevel cuts. To cut the bevel, you must position the rip fence where the blade will tilt away from it. With most saws, this means the fence must be shifted to the left side of the blade.

Some woodworkers use the rip fence unadorned to guide the bevel cuts, whereas others add a tall facing to it. I take a third tack, which is to use a holder that straddles the fence and slides along it. It's much like a home-made tenoning jig.

• The best way to set the blade tilt (and fence position) is against a layout of the bevel. Draw the bevel on the edge of a workpiece. Clamp the piece to the slide, raise the blade to the height of the fillet cut and tilt it to align with the layout. Sight across the blade to the layout.

• With the table saw set — blade at the correct height and angle, slide

Panels raised on the table saw lack a flat tongue to fit the panel groove in the frame. On the other hand, you can control the width and angle of the bevel, and you can produce a panel with or without the shoulder around the raised field.

straddling the fence — cut the bevels.

With a right-tilt table saw, it's often possible to stand beside the saw so you're behind the fence rather than at one end of it. You can pull the workpiece against the fence and slide it from right to left, making the cut.

If you have a left-tilt saw, as I do, then that stance isn't suitable. That's why the slide is beneficial. Clamp the panel to it with a couple of stiff spring clamps, and make each cut as you

would with a tenoning jig.

After four quick cuts the panel is formed. It still needs scraping and sanding to remove saw marks, but to this point the job has gone quickly, and the results are crisp and consistent.

A panel without a fillet around the field can be cut with one less step. Scribe the bevel layout on the edge of the workpiece, set the blade and cut. The initial sanding can be done quickly with a belt sander.

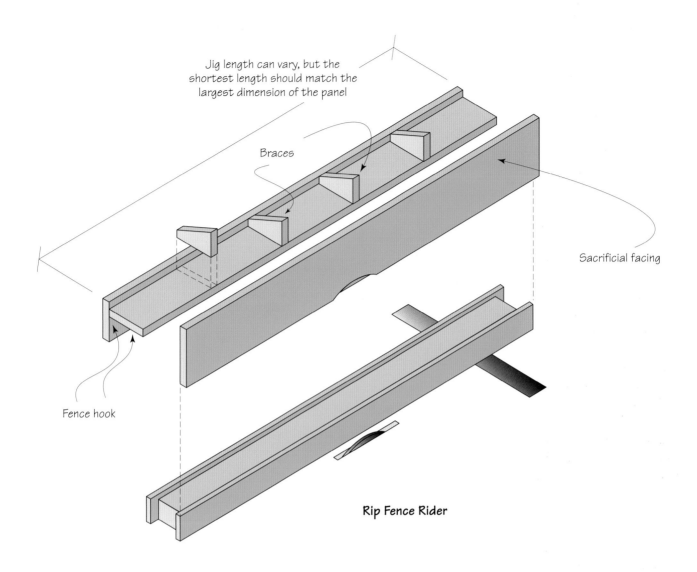

Jig length can vary, but the shortest length should match the largest dimension of the panel

Braces

Sacrificial facing

Fence hook

Rip Fence Rider

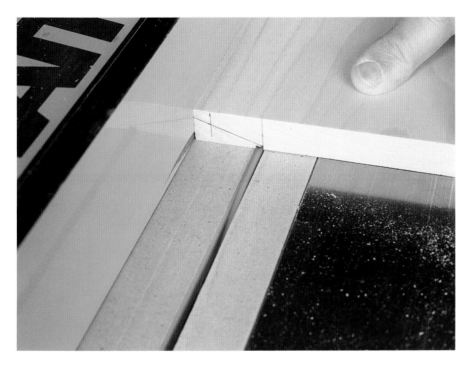

Assuming the panel is to have a shoulder around the raised field, the first operation is to kerf the face of the panel to define the shoulder. Set the blade to only $1/16$" high, and position the fence for the cut. Make four passes, scoring the face parallel to each edge.

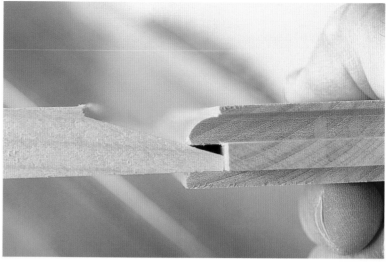

Lay out the bevel you want on the edge of a panel, and use it to set the blade height and angle. Stand the panel against the fence, and sight across the blade to the layout as you adjust the tilt, the height and finally the fence position. If you are using a slide to carry the panel through the cut, you must have it in place with your laid-out panel clamped to it for this setup process.

Make a test-cut, and fit the sample to the panel groove in an actual frame part. The trick in laying out the bevel is to angle it so the panel will be $\frac{1}{4}$" thick at the point $\frac{3}{8}$" in from the edge. This fitting will show whether you were successful. Be wary of a bevel that's a little too thick, because it can overstress the walls of the panel groove, causing them to crack or break completely.

Using a fence-mounted rider to feed the panel through the cuts is advisable. A plan for the rider I use is shown on page 77. Clamp the panel to the jig, and push it through the cut. The waste will fall benignly to the outside of the blade. Because you are clamping and unclamping each panel four times, use easy-to-apply clamps. The spring clamps shown above have enough force to hold the panel, yet a one-hand squeeze frees or secures the panel.

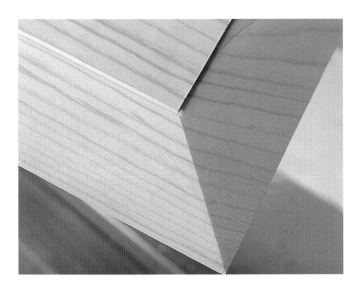

Although this freshly sawn panel doesn't look all that bad, it still displays the swirling saw marks typical of sawn bevels. Hand sanding will remove the marks and smooth the bevels. This panel will also need some touch-up work to remove the kerf marks at the corners of the raised field.

Along with the inevitable hand sanding, you may need to clean up the shoulders of the raised field. A rabbet plane works well for trimming scarring caused by the saw blade's teeth and for straightening up those shoulders.

CUTTING COVED PANELS ON THE TABLE SAW

Most woodworkers, I'm sure, are aware that coves can be cut on the table saw. Though the details of exactly how to do it may be murky to them, they know that it can be done.

How many of them realize that they can use that technique to form a panel cove? Let's dispel the murk.

You simply guide the workpiece across the blade at an angle — somewhere between 0° and 90° — to cut a cove. No special cutter is needed, though special cutters are available and do reduce the scraping and sanding needed after the cut. A standard rip or combination blade does the job.

To guide the work through the cut, use a fence set on a diagonal across the saw table. (Actually, to cut a full cove, you usually use two of these fences. To raise a panel, you use only half the cove, so you can use only one fence.) A shop-made device called a parallel rule (see "Parallel Rule" later in this chapter) enables you to determine the angle at which to set the fence(s). Deep-throated clamps secure these fences to the saw table.

Setting Up

To produce a panel cove, first determine how deep you want to cut and how wide the cove will be. For setup purposes, double the latter dimension.

For example: The panel stock is $5/8$" thick, and the panel groove in the frame pieces is $1/4$" wide and $7/16$" deep. To yield a $1/4$"-thick panel edge, the cove cut must be $3/8$" deep. To yield a 1" reveal, the cut must be $1\,7/16$" wide. Thus, the cut width for setup purposes is $2\,7/8$".

Mark the cut depth on the end of a stock scrap. Set the parallel rule to a width of $2\,7/8$".

First, set the blade height. Lay your marked scrap on the saw table, and adjust the blade height to line up the highest tooth with the deepest part of the cut.

All three panels were raised with coves cut on the table saw. Though somewhat tedious, the process allows you to create subtly unique coves for your raised-panel constructions. You can cut coves wider or narrower than the fixed form produced by a router bit or shaper cutter.

Next, find the fence angle. Place the parallel rule straddling the blade, and twist it left and right around the blade. What you need is the position at which both straightedges touch the blade simultaneously. It helps to move the blade by hand, so you can be sure the saw teeth are barely grazing the rule on both the infeed and outfeed sides.

When you've found the angle, you are halfway there. Mark the midpoint between the straightedges — that's the line on which you'll set your fence. Measure between the straightedges, and mark the midpoint at several places — well, at least two — along the parallel rule.

Clamp the fence to the saw table. Bear in mind that the blade is going to cut into the fence, so you should use something expendable. Crank the blade down below the saw table. Set the fence board on the line, and clamp it securely to the saw table. The fence should be on the infeed side of the saw table, that is, the fence should cover the front half of the blade. Work from the back of the saw.

If you reverse this setup, placing the fence across the outfeed side and working from the front of the saw, the blade will tend to pull the workpiece away from the fence. The spinning saw blade may just throw the workpiece in your face!

The hardest part of the whole setup may be locating the clamps.

Now you are ready to cut.

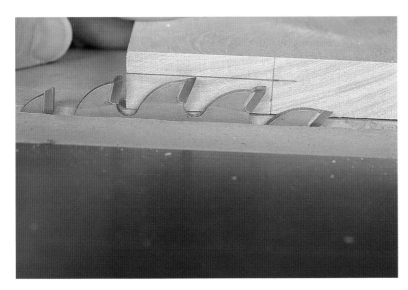

Setting the final blade height is the first task. On a scrap of the panel stock, lay out the depth of the cove you want to cut. The usual panel dimensions apply — you need a $\frac{1}{4}$"-thick tongue to fit in the frame's panel groove. On a $\frac{5}{8}$"-thick panel, the cove is $\frac{3}{8}$" deep. Place the scrap beside the blade, and adjust its height.

Dedicated Cove Cutter

There's a remarkable flexibility to cutting coves on a table saw. With a commonplace saw blade, you can achieve an infinite variety of cove forms — wide and shallow, narrow and deep, symmetrical or asymmetrical. You alter the angle at which the material passes over the blade to change the cove's width and its contour. Tilt the blade, and the range of contours expands dramatically.

The distinct drawback to using a table saw is the roughness of the completed cut. It can take a lot of scraping and sanding to get a smooth finish.

If you do a lot of coving, you may opt to invest in CMT's dedicated cove cutter. Designed by well-known furniture maker and teacher Lonnie Bird, the cutter is packaged with a selection of inverted-head router bits. The cutter features a heavy disk with fat, rounded carbide cutting tips that produce a very smooth finish. The cutter isn't cheap, but using it can eliminate a lot of onerous labor.

If you do a lot of custom coving, the cove cutter designed by Lonnie Bird and sold by CMT may be a worthwhile investment. Its primary benefit is that it produces a far smoother surface than your saw blade does. Compare the blade-produced cove on top to the cutter-produced cove under it. Both need some sanding, but the top one needs a lot of sanding.

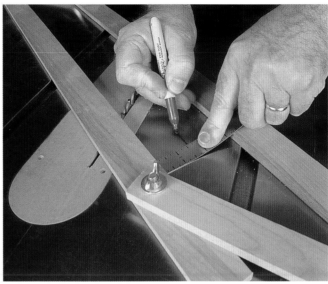

To find the angle for the fence, set the parallel rule to twice the width of cove you want on the panel. Straddle the blade with the rule, and pivot it, looking for the angle at which the saw teeth just graze the straightedges on either side. Turn the blade with your fingers as you adjust the rule's angle. It's a trial-and-error proposition.

You have the angle; now you must mark the position of the fence that will guide the cuts. For a panel cove, mark two points, one on either side of the blade and midway between the straightedges. I measure between them with a flexible rule and mark on the tabletop with a permanent marker (it comes off with turps).

Parallel Rule

The essential measuring device for coving on the table saw is the parallel rule. Make one with four strips of hardwood and four sets of stove bolts, washers and wing nuts. The critical job is drilling the holes. For the jig to work properly, the holes on each arm must be the same distance apart. The holes on each straightedge, or rule, must be the same distance from the guiding, or outside, edge. Tape the arms together when you drill them, and do the same when you drill the rules.

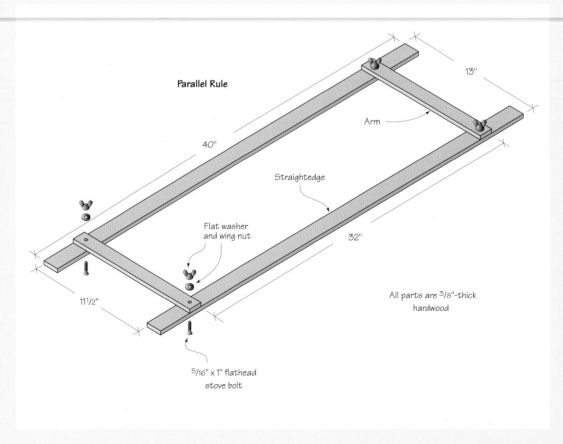

Parallel Rule

13"

Arm

40"

Straightedge

32"

Flat washer
and wing nut

11¹/₂"

All parts are ³/₈"-thick
hardwood

⁵/₁₆" x 1" flathead
stove bolt

Making the Cuts

Even though it is your table saw and you're used to making cuts in single passes on it, you have to work slowly to cut a cove. Make lots of passes, nibbling away to form the profile.

Raise the blade so it projects no more than ⅛" above the saw table. Use jointer-type push blocks to feed the workpiece. Press downward on the workpiece as you advance it.

The dangers in not applying enough downward pressure or in making too aggressive a cut — one with the blade set too high — is that the workpiece will ride up on the blade. That's kickback position: The teeth will grab the workpiece and throw it at you. Be very judicious in your cuts, and keep the pressure on.

Because you are raising a panel, you must run all four edges along the fence. Do an end first; end grain is most likely to tear out and splinter at the end of the cut. Then turn the panel and make a pass along a side. Do the second end, then the second side.

After the first pass, raise the blade a teensy bit. Make a second pass on all four edges. Raise the blade again, and make another pass. Just repeat the process again and again until you reach the final depth. Raise the blade only ¹⁄₁₆" for the final pass.

Coves cut this way definitely will need scraping and sanding. A curved scraper will remove the saw marks pretty quickly.

Cutting the cove isn't difficult, just tedious. You must go slow and steady. In effect, the blade scrapes off the waste. You must skim the surface, as you do with a cabinet scraper. Raise the blade in modest increments, and feed the stock slowly. You'll stand to the left-rear of the saw and feed diagonally toward the right-front. A push block grips the work better than you can with your bare hands, preventing slipping and mishaps.

Use something both straight and expendable for your fence (a strip of ¾"-thick MDF here). It's going to be right on top of the blade, and it will get cut. Lower the blade. Align the fence on the infeed side of your marks, and clamp it securely at each end.

This partially completed cove shows the effects of an overaggressive feed. Interestingly, the cross-grained cut is far smoother than the long-grain one, though the feed rate was probably the same for both cuts. Coarse sandpaper awaits.

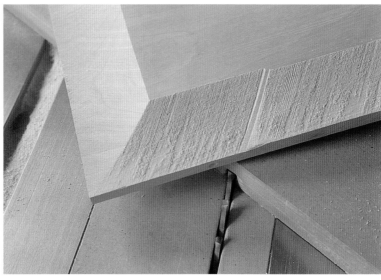

VENEERING PANELS

Veneering is the process of bonding thin pieces of wood to thicker substrates (or groundings). In frame and panel work, this method offers some excellent benefits.

The most obvious benefit is the range of woods, both domestic and exotic, that you can incorporate into your constructions. You can highlight your designs with spectacular wood figures and colors.

Beyond the aesthetic is the practical. Gluing a fragile wood, such as a burl, to a solid, stable substrate gives the fragile wood strength. Even better, the whole panel is dimensionally stable. You can use it as a structural part of the assembly. Glue it into the panel groove and reinforce the frame's strength.

Taking advantage of the benefits of veneering in frame and panel work doesn't require a lot of special equipment or any special skills. As you gain experience, you can branch out, of course, but what you need to know to start is pretty basic.

You need to make a press. You can use most any flat material for the press, but melamine has a plastic coating to which yellow glue doesn't bond well. That makes it less likely that glue squeeze-out will bond the panel to the press. I bought a quarter sheet of melamine at a home center, cut my press platens from it and had some left over.

When you place the freshly veneered panel between the press boards, use regular clamps to apply the pressure. Deep-throat clamps are a plus.

The best substrates for veneered panels are MDF and high-quality plywood. They are stable, flat and uniform — important characteristics in veneering. MDF especially is good because it has no grain orientation, so the veneer can be laid in any direction.

Always cut the substrate a little oversize — about a ½" all around is

Both flat and raised panels can be veneered. Veneering panels before raising them is a form of materials conservation: You produce four or five boffo panels from a single 5/4 board, which probably would yield only a single solid panel. Flat panels veneered with exotic woods and flamboyant figures can make an otherwise ordinary project a spectacular one.

plenty — so you can trim the veneered panel to accommodate minor veneer shifting that may occur when it gets pressed and to clean up the panel edges. In the same manner, cut the veneers to overhang the substrate by about ¼" all around.

The conventional wisdom is that you should balance the construction by applying veneer to both sides of the substrate. If you apply it to only one side, seasonal expansion and contraction of the veneer could distort the panel. This may be less significant when the panel is housed in a frame.

The veneering process is a gluing process. Apply glue — yellow or white will do just fine — to the substrate, never to the veneer. (If you apply glue to the veneer, it will curl up into a tube and be unusable.) Lay the veneer in place. Turn the piece over and veneer the back. Then quickly place the panel in the press, and apply the clamps. Wait four or more hours for the glue to cure. Open the press and release your beautiful veneered panel.

Veneers do need to be jointed before joining pieces edge to edge, just the way thicker boards do. A good way to do this is to press the leaves between two pieces of plywood or MDF with just $\frac{1}{16}$" protruding. I use stove bolts and plastic knobs to hold the two plies of the press together with their edges flush. Use a pattern bit or flush-trimmer bit in a router table to trim the protruding veneer clean and square.

The most obvious difference between commercial veneers and resawn veneers is their thicknesses. Commercial veneers — which are sliced, not sawn — are paper thin. You can't saw veneers that thin, and you probably wouldn't want to. Here slices of olive ash burl, maple and makore overlay resawn leaves of walnut and Spanish cedar.

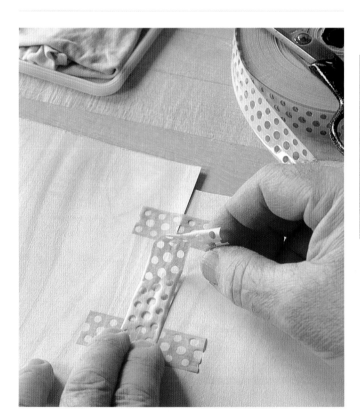

Although veneers produced by resawing — which are always thicker than purchased veneers — can actually be edge-glued, the standard way to join commercial veneers edge to edge is with thin paper veneer tape. Dampen the adhesive on the tape and stick it to the veneer, as shown above. The tape goes on the exposed face of the veneer. After the veneer is glued to its substrate, remove the tape with a cabinet scraper.

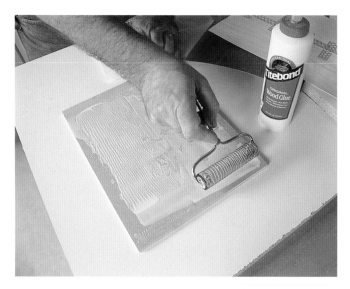

Yellow glue works fine for veneering in frame and panel work, but you can't dillydally. You can set your substrate panel — here a piece of $\frac{1}{4}$"-thick MDF — on the bottom platen of your veneer press. Have both the facing veneer and the backing veneer at hand. Squirt glue on the substrate, and spread it evenly with a printmaker's brayer (a hard rubber or plastic roller available in a variety of sizes and styles at art supply stores). This step is like painting with a roller.

Set the veneer onto the substrate, and press it into the glue. As it absorbs moisture from the glue, it will start to curl and ripple. The panel I'm working on in the photo above already has the veneer applied to its back. I've turned it over, spread glue on the face and started to set the veneer facing in place. The top platen of the press, just a piece of melamine, goes on next — and without delay.

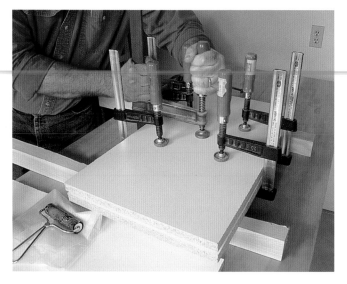

A small panel can be clamped between the pieces of melamine without extra cauls to distribute the clamping pressure if you use deep-throated clamps. The press is resting on lengths of 2x2 stock so it is easier to fit the clamp jaws under the press. Were the panel larger, I'd use cauls — lengths of $1\frac{1}{2}$" x 2" stock — in pairs to distribute clamping pressure.

Leave the veneered panel in the press about four hours — overnight is the oft-cited rule of thumb. When the clamps come off and the top is lifted, you'll have a beautiful panel, ready for trimming and finishing. Yellow glue could lightly stick to the melamine, but some light tapping or prying will break its bond.

Veneered Raised Panels

You can make raised panels that display highly figured grain. Highly figured stock — with crotches and burls, for example — is invariably the most expensive to buy and the most difficult to work.

Instead of milling figured boards down to ⅝" thick, resaw them into veneers. Glue these veneers to panels made of straight-grained pieces of the same stock, then raise the panels.

I won't detail how to resaw on the band saw, but I will point out that once you have the veneers cut, they must be surfaced. Planing veneers can be perilous, even for straight-grained veneers. Surfacing curly, burled or crotch-grained veneers is best done on a wide-belt sander or a drum sander. The ideal is to use the sander to smooth both the face and back of each leaf and, at the same time, reduce all to a uniform thickness just under ⅛".

The conventional wisdom is that you must veneer both the face and the back to balance a panel. (If you don't, the panel is likely to warp.) Here, the panel is trapped in a frame, which will prevent any warping, so it isn't absolutely necessary to veneer the panel backs.

Gluing these relatively thick veneers to solid-wood panels is done the same way commercial veneers are glued to sheet goods.

Be mindful of how raising the panels will parse or expose the thickness of the veneer and the substrate. You need a ¼"-thick tongue, and the raised field should be the thickness of the veneer. The seam between the substrate and the veneer will show if it falls on the bevel. Raise the panels before the final thickness sanding, sneaking up on the "disappearance" of the seam from the bevel. Then thickness-sand the panels to get the proper tongue dimension and to reduce the thickness of the raised field.

This panel is all walnut but not from the same boards. The face is a veneer cut from an expensive crotch-grained slab. The grounding (another name for substrate) is a glued-up walnut panel. The grounding's grain runs parallel to that of the veneer. The thickness of the veneer is evident in the inset. Overall, the panel is about ¾" thick, so it can be surfaced after it is raised to reduce both the thickness of the raised field and that of the panel tongue.

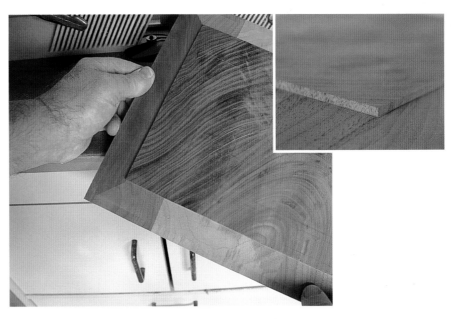

The usual panel-raising operation is completed in a pass or two. Raising this panel required a half dozen passes; I progressively raised the bit and cut deeper and deeper, until the seam between the veneer and the grounding "disappeared" into the shoulder of the field (inset). Yes, the panel would look even better if the boards making up the grounding had been better matched. (That's why this was the leftover panel.)

[CHAPTER *four*]

curved-edge frames and panels

Beyond the basic frame and beyond the divided frame with multiple panels are the frames with curved edges. Arch-topped doors come to mind immediately. These are highly popular on cabinets in kitchens, family rooms and dens. The concept isn't new: The so-called tombstone panel appeared on chests, secretaries and other furniture more than two centuries ago. French provincial armoires and buffets are notable for the complex curves on their rails and panels.

What is relatively new is the ease with which such assemblies can be made with a router. It is simply a matter of cutting the parts — usually the top rail and the panel — to the contour you desire, then using the pilot-bearing on the router bit, rather than the fence, to guide the cut.

Let me lead you through the making of a simple arch-topped door. Once you understand the process, you can apply it to making doors and casework assemblies. You can make assemblies with curves on the tops and bottoms, as well as on intermediate rails. Even the stiles can be shaped.

Large or small, with simple arches or undulating shapes, panels and doors with curved tops are special. As a bonus, construction is not difficult at all.

Curved-Topped Doors

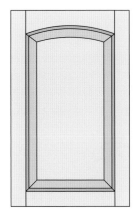
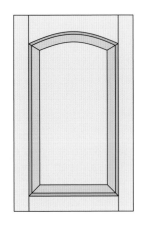
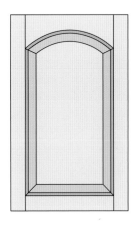
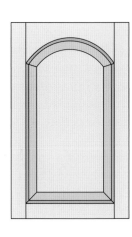

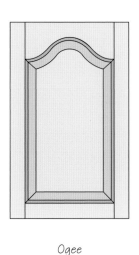
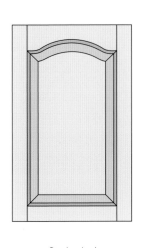
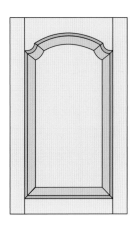
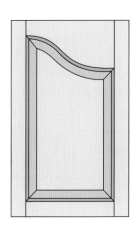

Ogee   Cathedral   Country   French provincial

Here are the principal steps:

1. Cut the parts, including the stiles and rails and the panel. This includes, of course, jointing and planing the stock, crosscutting the rails to final length and sizing the panel. The routine is just like making a standard door with straight rails.

2. Make the templates for the curve. You need one template for shaping the rail and one for shaping the panel. The rail template has a concave arc. The panel template has a convex arc. The radius of the panel's arc is $^{3}/_{8}$" longer than that of the rail's arc.

3. Cope the rails. Do this job the usual way. Chuck the bit in the router, adjust the height and set the fence tangent to the pilot-bearing guide. Make a cut across the ends of the rails, using a push block to guide the work along the fence.

4. Shape the curves. Saw off the bulk of the waste. Then, on the router table, flush-trim the rail to match the template.

5. Rout the sticking. Doing the stiles and the bottom rail is straightforward. For the curved top rail you can't use the fence; the cut is controlled by the pilot-bearing guide.

6. Raise the panel. This must be done using a horizontal bit. You cannot raise curved-edge panels with a vertical bit. Three of the panel's edges can be raised using the fence as a guide, but the curved edge must be raised using the pilot-bearing guide to guide the cut.

7. Assembly of the unit proceeds as if the rails and panel had only straight edges. If you want to cut the curved contour on the outside edge of the assembly, do it after it is glued up.

That's basically it, but let me flesh out the operation with details I think will be helpful.

TEMPLATES

Making templates obviates the need to reproduce a curve. Lay it out once, cut it once and smooth it once. Then you've captured it. With a template, you can knock out dozens of duplicate workpieces, each with the same curve and few needing more than light sanding. If you are producing multiples, templates can save you a lot of time.

You do need two templates. Using the same template for both the rails and the panels will not prove satisfactory. The radii of the arcs on these parts must be different, typically by $^3/_8$". That, of course, is because the panel extends beyond the rail's edge; it fits into the groove cut in the rail's edge.

For the templates to overlay the workpieces, you need to use a concave one on the rails and a convex one on the panels.

The templates can be made from plywood, MDF, hardboard, particleboard, and even plastic. Although I dislike the powder it becomes when sawn, routed and sanded, I prefer MDF for templates. It is cheap and flat. It forms a crisp edge, and fairing it is easy with coarse sandpaper and files.

Before you actually lay out and cut an arc, consider how you will attach each template to the wood. Common methods include carpet tape, small nails or hot-melt glue. Especially for multiples, I like to mount trap fences on the template because that makes it easy to swap workpieces and achieve a consistent alignment from part to part. I can even mount toggle clamps on the template so I don't have to fuss with tape or glue or leave marks, like nail holes, on the workpieces.

You do have to make the template large enough to accommodate the fences, of course, which is the reason for bringing up this matter now, before you actually make the templates. I use whatever scraps I find for the fences themselves. Short screws or brads attach the fences, and you can recycle the

screws after the jig's work is done. Lately I've been using a brad nailer to assemble jigs; it is really fast and effective.

An additional benefit of the extended template is that beginning and ending the cuts becomes safer and easier. With the extended template, I'm comfortable without a starting pin. Why? Because I can contact the pilot-bearing guide with the template while the work

is still clear of the bit's cutting edges. (If the template is the same length as the workpiece, the workpiece will be engaged by the bit's cutting edges before the template gets to the pilot-bearing guide. Control is a function of template-to-bearing contact. A starting pin gives you control in the split second at the beginning of a cut when you don't have template-to-bearing contact.)

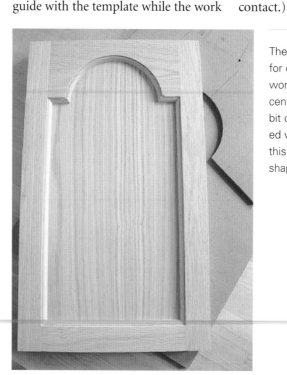

The tombstone shape, traditionally for doors and frame and panel casework, dates as far back as the 18th century. When the panel is raised, a bit of handwork is necessary. Updated with an oak plywood flat panel, this small tombstone door has the shape but not the handwork.

Curves aren't limited to the top of a door. This pair of doors has curves at the bottom as well as the top, and the line carries from door to door.

A template can be simple or elaborate, depending on how much use it'll get. At the simple end of the spectrum is the template with a center line to use in aligning the workpiece; attach it to the work with two or three brads (if the template will be on top for the cut) or carpet tape. A straight fence against which you set the rail's straight edge makes alignment of the work easier without the template having to be more complicated. Similarly, you can attach one or two fences to a panel template. Beyond that, you can add trap fences to consistently locate parts, and you can even use toggle clamps to secure parts quickly and securely.

Templates can be used again and again. Do you have to build a roomful of cabinets all with the same door size? Templates ensure all the doors are the same. Moreover, the templates don't need to be elaborate. The pair shown, made from scraps, have been in my collection for several years, and they still work.

Extend the guide edge of your template so it is longer than the actual cut. This allows you to bring just the template edge into contact with the bit's pilot-bearing guide to begin a cut. With the template against the bearing, you have control and can safely advance the workpiece so the cutting edges do their work.

The best template materials are readily available and cheap. You should choose something that's flat, has a firm edge and is easily cut. Here are some of the best choices: (bottom to top) Baltic birch plywood, ¼"-thick lauan or birch plywood, hardboard and different thicknesses of MDF. I favor the MDF: It's cheap, flat, void free, cuts easily (though its dust is awful) and has a crisp, durable edge.

Purchased Templates

Plastic templates for curved door parts are readily available. They are durable and work exactly as advertised.

You can buy sets for different door styles — simple arch, cathedral, country and so forth. The typical set consists of 8 to 12 concave templates for shaping rails and matching convex templates for shaping the panels.

For a big project — like a complete set of kitchen cabinets — that involves several door widths, the template sets can be a time-saver.

However, for a one-off project, you end up with one or two templates you use and 15 or 20 more that you don't. For the price you pay for the templates, you can buy a sheet of plywood or MDF to make the templates, and you'll have money left to buy a couple of new bits besides.

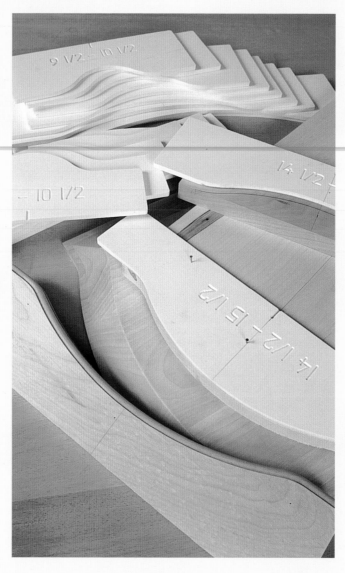

Plastic template sets for curved-edge frames and panels are sold by many bit vendors and general woodworking retailers. The typical set consists of templates for assemblies between 10" and 20" wide, and the contours are harmoniously proportioned. The templates are durable, with crisp, solid edges. Attach them to the workpieces with carpet tape or brads.

Cutting the Curve

How do you lay out and cut the templates? For me, it depends on the curve.

You can cut any curve on the band saw, then fair the edge with sandpaper and files. This process is generally easy for the woodworker with good band saw skills.

Before you can saw the line, though, you have to lay it out. If a simple arc is what you want (as opposed to a sinuous curve), a drawing bow may be a good layout tool. You get what is often called a "sprung curve."

The bow I use is a limber ripping with a short kerf sawed into each end. Catch a length of mason's cord in the kerfs, and knot it at one end. Flex the ripping to bow it, and capture the arc you want by pulling the free end of the string taut and tying it. Then you set the bow on your layout or workpiece and trace its arc with a pencil. If you have help close by, you can simply flex the bow and hold it in place while the helper traces the line. A third alternative is to clamp blocks outside the top corners of your layout and push the bow against them. Bend the bow to the line you want, then trace it yourself.

Don't know the radius of the curve you want? Don't even know what the curve looks like? Use the end points and a layout bow to draw it. The bow is a thin ripping, kerfed at each end for a bow string. Clamp scraps to the template on the end spots and use them as fulcrums in flexing the ripping. When you have a curve that looks good, capture it by looping the string through the kerfs. Then scribe along the bow onto the template. You can scribe several different lines and choose the one that looks best to you.

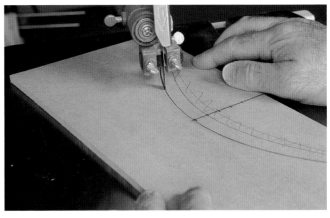

Cut the chosen curve. Those with impeccable band saw skills can cut to the line. Those of us who have less confidence will saw shy of the line, then file and sand to it.

Fair the sawn edge. A fair curve is smooth and even, without flat spots and random undulations. A large-diameter drum or spindle sander can make quick work of evening out the curve. Lacking that, try the half-round side of a cabinetmaker's rasp, which is smoother than a regular wood rasp but coarser and faster cutting than a regular file. Sweep from one end to the other rather than working isolated spots along the edge.

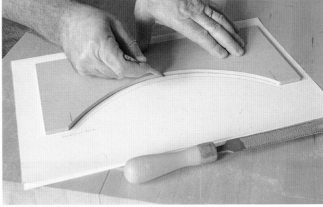

Monitor your progress toward a smooth, even curve by tracing the template edge onto paper and looking at the pencil line. Subtle flats and bumps that you don't see when looking at the template edge will jump out at you when traced onto paper.

Trammel-Routing a Curve

If you're skeptical of your ability to saw a fair curve freehand, you can use a router and trammel to create many types of curves. A router and trammel make it easy to cut matched pairs of templates for shaping rails and panels.

The easiest is the fixed-radius arc. But with care, you can rout ogees and even cathedral, country and French provincial curves. You have to set up several pivot points for each template, and some handwork may be necessary at the transition points.

The radii of an arched rail edge and its matching panel edge are slightly different: The panel's radius is actually $3/8$" longer. This is easy to lay out with a compass but difficult to achieve freehand. That's why I prefer to use a trammel to make templates. The router trammel is a compass with a cutter instead of a pencil.

Rout a matched pair of templates from a single piece of template stock — here ¼"-thick birch plywood. Make the rail template first. Scribe a line down the center of the blank. Mark the crest of the arc on this line, leaving yourself plenty of space for the workpiece and any fences you plan to attach to the template. From the crest measure off the radius, and drill a pivot hole through the blank. To protect your bench top, stick the blank to a sacrificial piece of plywood (mine has seen a lot of use).

Set up the router and trammel, then cut the arc. When you set the radius, be sure to include the bit in the measurement. Set the plunge depth to the thickness of the template stock. Swing the router back and forth on the pivot, cutting through the stock in two to four passes. The template in this photo is clamped, but the whole blank is stuck to the sacrificial panel with carpet tape. Neither the template nor the pivot should shift when the two separate.

In theory, both the panel and rail arcs share a center point. In practice, you have to shift the pivot for the panel. From the crest of the first cut, measure at least $^{3}/_{8}$" along the center line. From that mark, measure the panel radius and drill a new pivot hole.

Reset the trammel's radius, and cut the panel arc. Remember that for this cut the bit is outside the radius. The plunge depth remains the same, of course. As before, you should cut the arc in two or four passes.

Here are your basic templates. The crests of the arcs are $^{3}/_{8}$" apart when the tips meet. You can use these templates as they are, or you can brad or screw fences to them to simplify mounting the parts for shaping.

SHAPING THE PARTS

With the templates in hand, you are almost ready to shape the parts. The task remaining before you do that is to cope the ends of the rails. Coping them after they are shaped is asking for the acute tips to be blown off, so cope them first.

Before you go any further, set up the sticking cutter and rout the sticking profile on support strips to nest into the copes. These strips will support the acute tips as they are roughly cut on the band saw, then shaped to match the template. They'll continue to support the fragile tips as you rout the sticking. (See "Supporting the Tips" later in this chapter.)

If you've done any template work, you know you should trim the workpiece to match the template. If there's a lot of waste to cut away, you do just that: Cut it; don't rout it.

Place the template on the coped rail or the panel. Trace the arc onto the workpiece. Remove the template, and saw off the bulk of the waste with a band saw or a jigsaw. Stay to the waste side of the line, of course, but try to stay within $\frac{1}{16}$" or $\frac{1}{8}$" of it to reduce the amount of material you'll have to rout away.

Flush-trim the rail or panel to match the template, usually — but not always — doing the job on the router table. For this, you should bond the template to the workpiece using carpet tape, brads, hot-melt glue or the like.

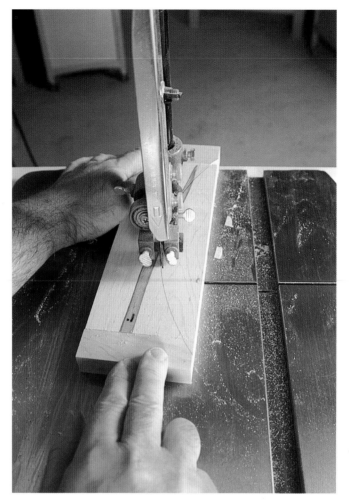

Before roughing out the shape on the band saw (you can do this with a jigsaw, of course), cope the rail ends and make sticked supports to nest into the copes. Use the template to scribe the arc onto the workpiece, including those supports. Then saw close to the line.

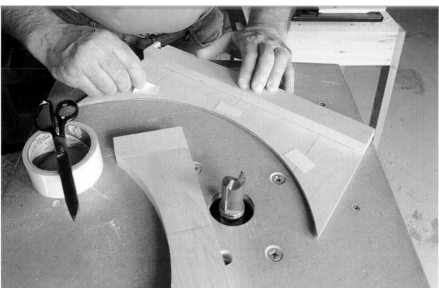

Mount the rough-cut part on the template to shape it with a router. Don't rely on fences to keep the part in place. Fences will locate the part on the template, but unless it is held down, the part can creep forward into the cutter or lift from the template. Two or three patches of carpet tape will secure the part. I recommend using fresh patches for each part. Note that if placed right, the carpet tape can hold the backup scraps in place on the coped ends of the rail.

Paso Robles Pattern Set

Pattern bits are the ones with a bearing mounted on the shank (as opposed to the tip). Most manufacturers have them in various sizes and lengths. Paso Robles Carbide has a unique five-bit template set that provides sensible capabilities for the serious router woodworker. All five bits have $1/2$" shanks, and the cutter lengths and diameters are proportioned to ac-commodate templates between $1/4$" and $3/4$" thick and workpieces up to $1^1/2$" thick.

The usual routine is to cut the workpiece to within $1/8$" of the template contour, then rout it to match the template perfectly. The difficult part is cutting close to the line without cutting beyond it. To be safe, we usually err toward the waste side, leaving a lot more than $1/8$" for the router to trim. That makes for a heavy cut, which dulls bits quickly and increases the risk of tear-out.

The template-bit set has two bits with slightly over-size bearings. These do the heavy labor of reducing the workpiece contour to within $1/16$" of the template. You then use a flush-trimmer bit from the set to make a clean final pass.

Five bits are included in the Paso Robles pattern bit set. The bit in the center is the loner, a $3/4$"-diameter pattern bit with a $1/2$" cutting length. The others are paired for two-stage template work. One bit in each pair has an oversize bearing; the other has a bearing matched to the cutting diameter. The larger pair (at left) have $1^1/8$" cutting diameters with $1^5/8$" cutting lengths. The smaller pair have $3/4$" cutting diameters and $7/8$" cutting lengths.

This bit has a bearing that's $1/8$" larger than its cutting diameter. Use this one first to trim the workpiece to within $1/16$" of the template.

For the final pass, switch to the bit with the bearing diameter that matches the cutting diameter.

Routing with the Templates

If you use a straight pattern bit, the template needs to rest on the tabletop with the workpiece on top of it. With a flush-trimmer bit, you must have the template on top of the workpiece. Use a starting pin to brace the workpiece as you begin the cut, and feed in the proper direction (generally left to right, or if the workpiece is between you and the bit, right to left).

If you are new to this operation, you might benefit from a practice run or two using spare pieces. Depending on the grain of the wood you work and the line of the arc, you might run into chipping, even chunking, when you move from long grain into end grain and the rotation of the bit conflicts with the "nap" of the grain. The cutting edges want to lift the grain rather than lay it down. Occasionally, the edge will grab some grain and yank, jerking the work, making a grim noise and scaring the daylights out of you. In some cases, the edge will be damaged beyond repair.

You can usually circumvent this problem by routing the contour in two steps. Rout halfway, then flop the workpiece on the template and rout the second half. Both cuts are made "downhill." An alternative approach is to rout one half with a pattern bit and the other half with a flush-trimmer bit. Orient the template down for the first cut, then turn over the template and workpiece to cut the second half. This method can be an nuisance unless you have two router tables (well, some of us do!) and can move from one to the other instead of having to change bits over and over.

Trimming a curved rail flush with the template is a standard pattern-routing operation. The bearing on the bit's shank rides along the template, and the bit trims off any material projecting beyond the template edge. If you have a choice, a large-diameter bit (such as the one in use here) is better than a small-diameter one for pattern routing because the larger diameter reduces the angle at which the cutting edge addresses the wood. The lower the angle, the less chance there is of chipping and tear-out.

Whenever you rout across the grain, you risk this sort of damage. In this instance, the work was facedown with the template on top, and the bit's cutting edges were sweeping obliquely across end grain, against the "nap," on the downhill side of the arc. As the cut carried close to the straight edge of the workpiece, there was nothing behind the wood fibers to hold them in place. A substantial shard simply split away along the grain, and the rail is now scrap.

An effective tactic to avoid workpiece destruction when shaping curves is to always rout downhill, so the cutting edges sweep across the grain on the descent side of the curve. Do this by using a pattern bit on one half the curve (left) and a flush-trimmer bit on the other (right). The work remains bonded to the template throughout; you turn the whole works over when you switch bits. Note that the work-piece and template get fed in the same direction for both cuts, which is from my right to my left, and both cuts move downhill. (This is most efficient if you have two router tables and can set up a different bit in each.)

Using a handheld router is a sensible way to shape duplicate curved-edge parts. You can safely feed the router in either direction to avoid chipping and tear-out. If the template is fitted with trap fences to locate the part, the weight of the router on top will keep the part in place, so you don't need to tape it down. This expedites the swapping of workpieces when you are in a high-production mode. Moreover, if the work isn't stuck down, you can do half the contour, then flip the piece over and rout the second half. No climb-cutting is required to avoid chipping and tear-out. To work with a handheld router effectively, though, you have to make the template large enough to place clamps clear of the router's path. You also must be sure that the cutter or bearing won't damage your bench top.

Trap fences on something like a panel template can be deceiving and make you think they're immobilizing the workpiece. The cutting forces *will* push the workpiece away from the guiding edge, and you won't get an accurate contour. Applying a clamp across the fences and panel will keep the panel in place throughout the cut.

Toggle clamps are excellent for high-production template work. They'll hold the work securely but allow you to swap workpieces quickly. In addition, they act as handgrips for maneuvering the template and working past the bit. Just make the template and fence wide enough to accommodate them.

STICKING THE CURVE

Stick the curved edge with the same bit and setup as the straight edges. You just can't use the fence. Except at the beginning and end, the cut has to be controlled by the bit's pilot-bearing guide. The fence literally will be in the way.

The pilot-bearing guide rides on the workpiece, not the template, so you don't use the template at all.

To safely begin the cut, you need to use a starting pin. The explanation for this bears repeating. As you begin a bearing-controlled cut, the cutting edges of the bit engage the wood first. In that split second, the cutter can flick the wood off to the right. Best case: The cut is botched. Worst case: Your fingers tangle with the cutter.

The starting pin gives you leverage. You brace the work against the pin, then lever it against the bit. Once the wood contacts the bearing, you can come off the pin if you want. Feed the workpiece through the cut. Although the same dynamic (the cutting edges, but not the pilot-bearing guide, being engaged with the wood) applies at the end of the cut,

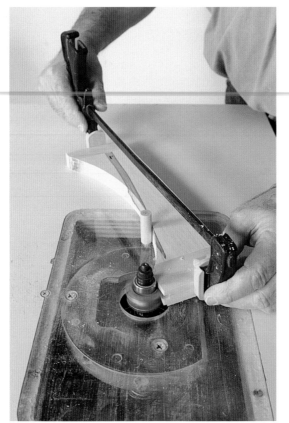

it is much less likely to be problematic. You can use a pin on the outfeed side of the bit to maintain control as the work clears the bit.

Routing without the fence may seem like freehand, but only until the workpiece comes into contact with the bit's pilot-bearing guide. The starting pin is a device that tempers the "free" part, giving you leverage as you swing the tip of the work onto the spinning bit. (The clamp holds the supports tucked into the copes on either end of the rail, and it doubles as a grip.)

Without the fence, the bit is fully exposed, and it is a good idea to use a guard.

As you stick your first curved rail, you'll realize how effective the fence is at collecting dust. Without the fence, the dust will spew across the tabletop. The sort of bit guard shown in some photos will capture a lot of it. (You may be able to buy something like it if you don't want to make it.)

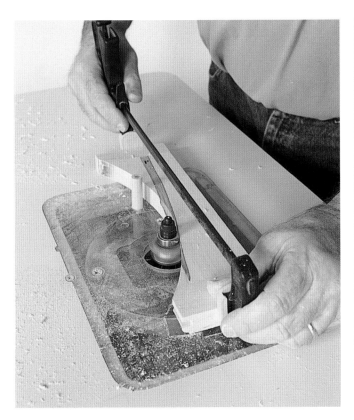

Once the pilot-bearing guide is engaged, you can drift the work off the starting pin; its work is done. As you continue the cut, the bearing is in control. Note the way the chips are dispersed across the tabletop without any sort of guard or pickup.

End the cut simply by sliding the work off the bearing. A benefit of the supports clamped to the rail ends is protection of the piece as it comes off the bearing. There's a tendency for the trailing end of the work to follow the bearing, which often results in a dip or snipe in the sticking profile. With the support in place, it takes the hit instead of the rail.

Using a Starting Pin

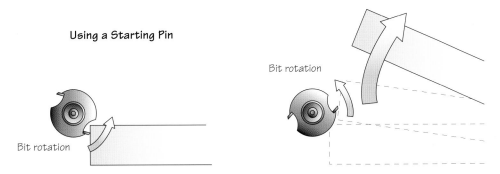

Bit rotation

Bit rotation

Workpiece is caught by cutting tip of spinning bit before it reaches the pilot bearing. This happens in a nanosecond!

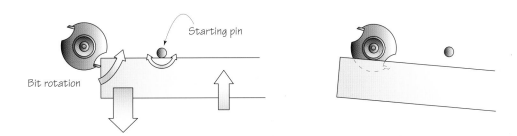

Starting pin

Bit rotation

The starting pin gives leverage to counter the rotational force of the bit. Maintaining contact with the starting pin isn't necessary after the work contacts the pilotbearing.

Supporting the Tips

Depending on the steepness of the arc, the sticking cut may break out the tip of the rail as it exits the cut — very bad, of course. Even if the chip is minor, which it usually is, it will mar the quality appearance you are working hard to achieve.

To prevent this chipping, you need to support the fragile corner. Stick a scrap to mate with the cope, as shown in many of the photos in this section.

Tuck that support into the cope before you shape the blank. Trim it with the template so it blends into the curved edge. Then when you cut the sticking, you'll have solid material backing up the wood at the fragile end of the cut, as well as stock to maintain contact with the pilot-bearing guide and carry the workpiece safely past the cutter.

Bad endings to the sticking cuts mar the tips of these curved rails, proof that supporting the copes throughout the shaping and sticking process is worthwhile. With nothing backing up the work, the tip of the arched rail split away. It's a tiny flaw; how picky are you? The cathedral rail has a little dip in the profile because I didn't guide the piece cleanly off the pilot-bearing guide at the cut's end, a common goof. With a support block in the cope, the dip would have been in that block, not the rail.

The use of some form of bit guard is always advisable when making bearing-guided cuts. This shop-made guard mounts to the tabletop with a long bolt that extends through the nose of the wooden side into the starting pin hole (and a clamp on an extension at the tabletop edge). That nose serves as the starting pin. The shop vacuum hose captures a lot of the dust but not all of it. The clear plastic top extends over the bit. It works in all phases of this work: pattern routing, sticking and panel raising.

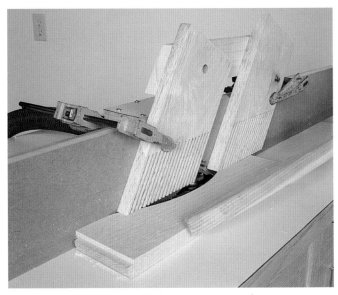

Rails that have straight sections flanking the curve can be profiled in two stages. Use the fence, complete with featherboards, to control the sticking of the straight sections (right). Then swing the fence clear of the bit, and complete the full edge using the pilot-bearing guide.

Using a Curved Fence for Rails

A curved fence is an option for sticking rails — and raising panels, as we'll see — that may suit you better than depending on the pilot-bearing guide. Even if you are comfortable with bearing-guided cuts, you may find the curved fence to be the appropriate way to handle specific cuts.

The curved fence won't work for every curve, of course. The contour must be a fixed-radius arc — no undulating or multiradius contours. If the radius is short, as it usually is on a tombstone shape, the fence has to be a disc.

What are the benefits?

Safety and comfort are primary. The bit is shrouded in the fence, so you don't feel exposed to the cutting edges. The workpiece follows a fixed path through the cut; that may feel more secure to you, and that sense is important.

Using a fence allows you to stage the cut. You can make a shallow scoring cut first, then complete the profile in a couple of additional passes.

Finally, you can moderate the depth of the cut if you need to. An example is an unembellished door being constructed with groove-and-stub-tenon joinery. Slotting cutters make a ½"-deep cut. With a curved fence, you can reduce that cut on the arched rail to ⅜" to match the grooves made in the stiles and straight rail.

If there's a drawback to a curved fence, it's that this fence is job specific. Every radius arc requires its own fence.

Although some woodworkers use a band saw to cut the arc for a curved fence, I prefer to cut it with a trammel-guided router. The radius is the same as that for the rail, but the bit must be outside the radius when you cut the fence (it's inside the radius when you cut the rail template). Size the fence blank so it'll extend close enough to the tabletop edge to be clamped. Here, my MDF blank is taped to my sacrificial benchtop cover. The pivot point is in a scrap block butted to the edge of the blank.

Bore an opening in the edge of the fence for the bit. Obviously, the hole must be large enough to accommodate the bit with a little adjustment clearance, and it must break through the curved edge. A Forstner bit makes this kind of hole easily.

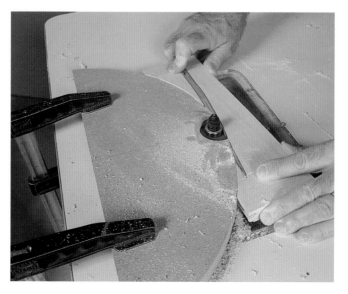

Locate the fence tangent to the bearing and clamp it. The bearing is on top, so you can easily use a rail as a setup guide to position the fence. My table has the router offset toward the front, so I have the fence clamped at the front of the table, and I work from the back.

RAISING THE PANEL

Raising a panel with a curved edge is the supreme operation. For a lot of woodworkers, this operation is the justification for the top-of-the-line table, the mammoth router, and the precision adjuster.

You can't do this particular operation with a vertical bit (which can be run at full router speed and doesn't require as much power). You have to do it with a big horizontal bit, meaning that you need a high-horsepower, variable-speed router.

The curved edge(s) must be raised using the bearing on the bit to guide the cut. You can use a curved fence for a panel with a simple arch but not complex ones, and the regular fence is of no use for any curves. The bearing, on the other hand, works for any contour.

The generally accepted sequence is to raise the curved edge first. Typically, you will rout across the grain, and as the cut is completed, the wood fibers will tear out. The well-established remedy for this cross-grained blowout is to do the cross-grained cut first; the subsequent cut along the grain will eliminate the torn-out fibers.

With the curved edge raised, move the fence into position, and use it to guide the raising of the straight edges. Do a long-grain edge, then the cross grain, and finish up with the second long-grain edge.

Use a starting pin when raising the curved edge of a panel. Brace the panel against the pin, then twist it into the bit to begin the cut. Once the bit's bearing engages the edge of the panel, you can come off the pin. Use a push block to hold the panel down on the tabletop, and at the same time advance the panel through the cut. Don't dillydally; a slow feed will scorch susceptible wood, like cherry and maple. There's no need for an ending pin to help you maneuver the panel off the bit, though you certainly can set up and use one. All you do is keep the panel moving, right off the bit.

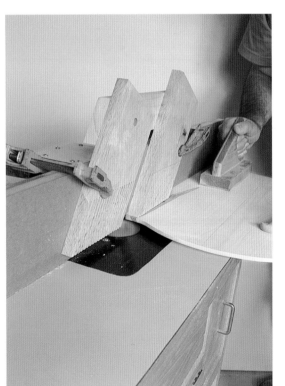

Once the panel is raised along the curved edge, you can, without changing the bit, set the fence in place to raise the three straight edges. Use featherboards and the appropriate push block.

Staging the Cut

Using the bearing to control the cut impacts the cut volume. As we've seen, when doing straight edges you can use either the bit height or the fence position to limit the amount of material removed in a pass.

In this situation, it seems, you have only the bit elevation to limit the volume of material removed in a pass.

Obviously, you should have a consistent depth all the way around the panel. By doing the curved edge first, you can work to the final depth through a series of progressively deeper cuts. Have the bit low for the first pass, then raise it progressively for subsequent cuts. Once you have the curved edge cut to final depth, hold that bit height. Move the fence into position for cutting the straight edges, and use the fence position to limit the cut volume. (This approach won't work with a bit equipped with a back-cutter.)

Another option is to swap bearings. If you have a super-duper rabbeting set with one bit and a handful of bearings, you can use the largest of those bearings on your panel-raising bit to moderate the cut. Keep in mind that you have to make a big jump in bearing diameter to have much impact on the cut width. Using a $^3/_4$"-diameter bearing instead of the usual $^1/_2$" diameter is almost meaningless.

No rabbeting set? Bearings from your set don't fit your panel-raising bit? Most bit vendors sell individual bearings. Order one with the correct inside diameter and a large — say $1^3/_8$" — outside diameter.

The cut width can be limited by using a large-diameter bearing on your panel-raising bit instead of the standard bearing. This reduces the stress of a heavy cut on both your tools and on you. In this instance, the bearing is the largest from a set provided with a rabbetting bit.

After the first pass on the curved edge of all your panels, back out the mounting screw and remove the large bearing. If you want to stage the cut further, select and mount a different bearing. Two stages are enough for you? Remount the standard bearing. Don't forget the slinger, a washerlike spacer typically used between the bit stem and the bearing. Without it, the bearing can jam against the cutter, resulting in a scorched edge on your workpiece.

The difference in the volume of waste removed in the two cuts is evident when you compare the single-pass cut (top) to the two-pass cut (bottom).

Bearing-Guided Circumnavigation

As often as not, when a panel has a curved edge, I cut all four edges with the bearing as the guide. Begin with the curved edge, and as you reach the corner, just make the turn and continue to cut along the straight edge. Turn the next corner and rout across the bottom edge. Turn again and finish the panel. All the panel's edges need to be crisp and dingfree for this method to produce good results.

More important, you have to be comfortable with the operation. For me, it works well so long as the panel isn't too big. If the procedure makes your palms sweaty, take a time-out, then try a different cut sequence.

Circumnavigating a panel begins at the starting pin, against which you brace the panel so you can begin cutting the curved edge. The bit should be spinning at the router's lowest speed setting. Pivot the panel on the starting pin until the edge contacts the bearing. Use a push block to advance the panel's edge along the bearing.

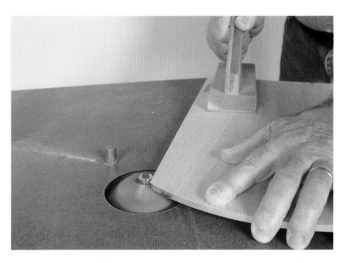

As the corner of "curve" and "straight" approaches the bearing, shift the push block and maneuver the panel around the corner. Then feed the panel along the bit, cutting the long-grain straight edge.

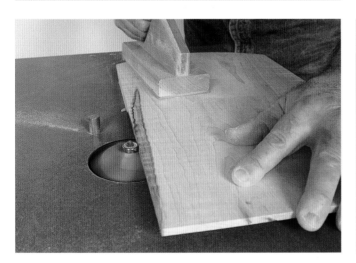

At the second corner, between the side and bottom edges, swing the panel and rout across the bottom, raising it. Swing again at the third corner, and head back toward the top of the panel. End the cut at the final corner by continuing the feed to carry the panel off the bearing and the bit.

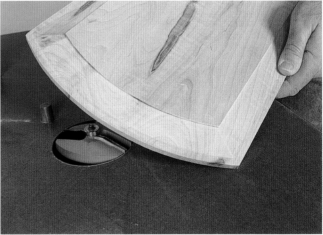

There's no difference in appearance between a panel raised in a continuous operation guided by the bearing and done with care and one done partly with the bearing and partly with the fence. However, the continuous operation is a much quicker method.

Using a Curved Fence for Panels

Just as you can use a curved fence to guide sticking cuts on rails with fixed-radius curves, you can do it with panels. The difference is that the panel fence must have a concave arc, not a convex one.

As with the fence for sticking the rails, the curved panel fence has limitations. It works with fixed-radius arcs, but that's it. On the plus side, it does allow you to stage cuts, and it does shroud the bit, reducing your exposure to its cutting edges.

Make the curved fence in the same way as you made the rail fence. Cut it with a router and trammel. Use the same radius for the fence as you did for the panel template, but pull the bit inside the radius. Make the fence long enough to span the router table's top. The panel-guiding curve will take a bite out of the edge. You don't need to bore a bit opening as large as a horizontal bit; just make it larger than the bearing.

Clamp the fence across the tabletop; center the bit in the arc. Adjust the fence so the guiding edge is tangent to the bit. With the bit spinning, raise the cutter to the appropriate height for raising your panels. This will hog out a clearance recess in the underside of the fence.

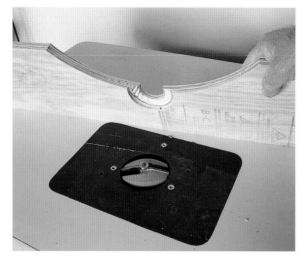

The fence is a strip of construction plywood with the appropriate arc routed into it. Though the bit is 3½" in diameter, you need bore only a 1"- to 1½"-wide opening for it. With the fence clamped in place, switch on the router and raise the bit so it routs clearance for itself in the underside of the fence.

The best way to align the fence with the pilot-bearing is to use a panel. Locate the fence and clamp one end to the tabletop. Hold the panel in the fence's hollow, and swing the fence fore and aft to bring the panel edge against the bearing and also tight against the fence. Without moving the fence, set the panel aside and clamp the fence's free end.

Usher the panel through the raising cut with a twisting movement. Except at the beginning and the end of the cut, the bit is shrouded by the panel and the fence, quite different from the usual exposure when using the bearing alone to guide the cut.

TOMBSTONE PANELS

Characterized by a pronounced arch that has flat shoulders on either side, the tombstone shape is one of my favorites. In the 18th century, cabinetmakers used it in a variety of frame and panel applications, especially in doors. Chapter one includes a photo of a lidded chest I made based on one built in the 1760s. It has two narrow tombstone panels in front, twin focal points in a four-panel front assembly.

Tombstone panels require extra work to shape and raise. Some of that is handwork, but it's worth the extra effort, in my book.

There are several traditional types of tombstone doors. What varies from type to type is the location of the arch's center point. Three of the types are shown in the drawing on the next page. In the most common type, usually called the standard, the center is on the shoulder line of the raised field. In this type, the arch is less than 180°. In another style, the center falls on the line of the sticking's shoulder, so the arch is higher and the panel has straight drops from the arch to the shoulder.

Traditional tombstone assemblies are built with mortise-and-tenon joints and mitered sticking. That's where I depart from tradition. I've built them with contemporary cope-and-stick joinery. In tall doors, which are heavy and thus put great stress on the joinery, I reinforce the joints with loose tenons, as detailed in chapter two.

Whatever style you choose to make, take the time to draw a full-size plan and prepare a detailed parts list. In the following pages, I show you how to build the tombstone door shown here.

In a nutshell, the construction begins with a pair of complementary templates: one for the panel, the other for the top rail. You use the templates first to lay out the parts, then to shape them. You can even use the rail template as the holder when you rout the sticking.

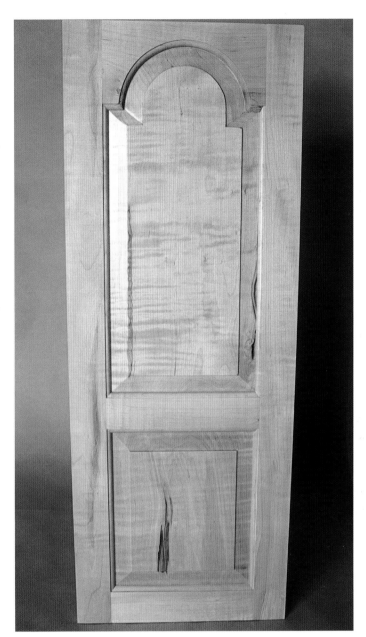

The tombstone door is an enduring and distinctive type of curved-edge design. The traditional construction is often a time-consuming process, but you can use cope-and-stick joinery to reduce the labor without sacrificing strength.

The rails are coped, the top rail is shaped and all the frame parts are sticked.

The panel is shaped and raised next. Detailing the arch and its shoulders is where the handwork comes in. Relax — it's not that difficult. Practice on a sample made of inexpensive material. After shaping a bevel or two, you'll feel more confident about tackling a "real" project made from good wood.

Designing a Tombstone Door

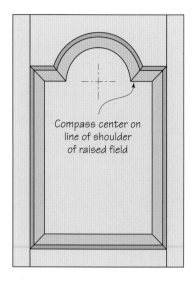

Compass center on line of shoulder of raised field

Standard

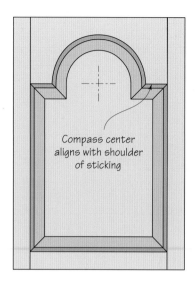

Compass center aligns with shoulder of sticking

Straight-sided

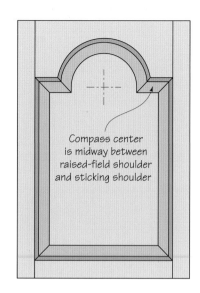

Compass center is midway between raised-field shoulder and sticking shoulder

Pinched

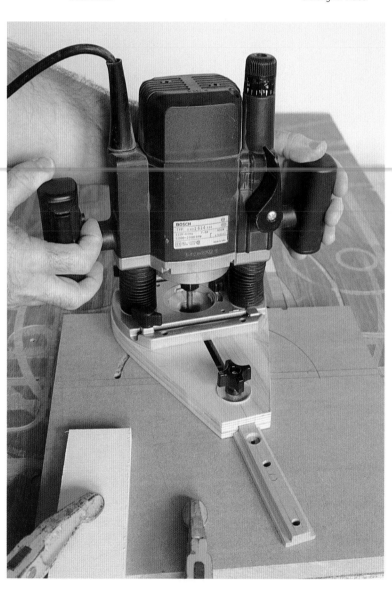

With plan in hand, begin work on the tombstone door by making templates for the top rail and the panel. The panel template is more demanding to cut, because the shoulders flanking the arc must be square to the sides and the arc must be stopped at the shoulders. Lay out the shoulders, locate the arc's center and scribe the arc with a compass. Set the trammel's pivot, and place the router on the work. Before cutting, swing the router through the arc and clamp a stop to the template to prevent the router from edging past the shoulder as it cuts. In the setup shown, the clamps holding the blank and the sacrificial plywood under it interfered with the trammel's arm, so the arc was cut one half at a time. After routing the arc, cut the shoulders on the table saw with the template on edge in the miter gauge. Then tack on fences to locate the panel.

Rout the copes on the rails, then use the template to shape the top one. Saw away the half circle of waste with a jigsaw or a band saw. Tuck the rail in the template, and secure it with a couple of carpet tape patches. To avoid problems with tear-out, shape only half the arc with a pattern bit (left). For this cut, the template is on the bottom. Switch to a flush-trimmer bit, turn the piece over so the template is on top and cut the second half of the arc (right).

Rout the sticking next. Set up the bit and stick the stiles and any other rails, using the fence and featherboards to control the operation. While the bit is in place, stick the short flats that flank the rail's arch. Without moving the bit, clear the fence from the table and stick the arch. You don't need the starting pin in this instance because the two flats have already been cut. You can engage the bit and bearing via one of them (the one on the left). Dip around the corner into the arch, and rout the profile from one end to the other.

An alternative approach to the sticking cut is available. If you are uncomfortable with the idea of using your hands directly on the rail to maneuver it through the cut, use the template as a holder. The rail, at least in the instance shown above, is pretty small. Set the rail on the top of the router table, then place the template over it. The template is a bit of a buffer between the cutting and your hands.

Turn to the panel. Begin shaping it by laying it on the template and scribing the top-edge contour. Cut the straight shoulders on the table saw. Raise the blade to the height of the shoulder. Support the panel on edge with an extended facing attached to the miter gauge. Line up the panel for the first shoulder cut, and set a stop against the bottom end of the panel, clamping it to the miter gauge extension. Cut the first shoulder, then roll the panel, butt it against the stop and cut the second shoulder.

You can shape the panel either on the router table or with a hand-held router. The advantage in the latter approach lies in your ability to cut half the arch by feeding the router in the correct direction (left to right) and to avoid chipping by climb-cutting the other half of the arch. (This is not a safe procedure on the router table. The router is stationary and the work is moving. If the bit grabs, which it can in climb-cutting, the work may be snatched from your grasp and fired off the table. Startled, you could tangle with the now exposed bit. In the handheld situation, the work is stationary; the result of a grab by the bit is to jerk the router, which is startling but not so hazardous.)

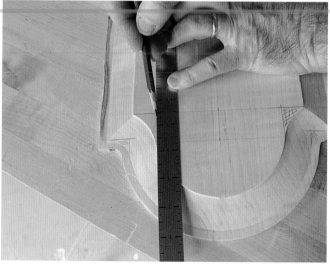

Raise the panel on the router table. Cut the top contour first, using a starting pin to begin the cut safely. A push block is a safe means to both feed the panel and apply downward pressure to it.

The handwork begins once the panel is raised. If you are primarily a power tool woodworker (like me), this task may seem daunting. But sharpen your chisels and do this little bit of paring. Lay out the square shoulders of the raised field to begin. Pencil a line across the field from outside corner to outside corner, then extend a tangent from the arch perpendicular to the penciled shoulder line. Also lay out the sharp inside corner where the bevel and tongue come together.

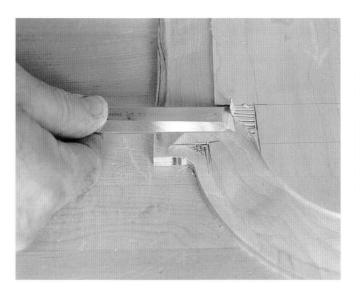

Chop out the waste from the inside corners using your bench chisels. The shoulder of the field was defined by the panel-raising cuts. Hold that depth as you pare the waste.

Use a small rule and a knife to slice a line from the inside corner of the field to the inside corner at the edge of the panel. This is the junction between the planes of the bevel.

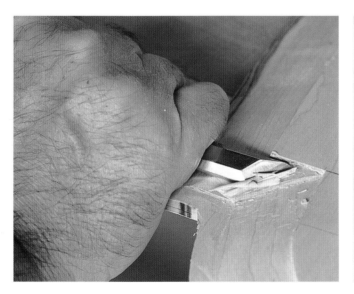

Use left- and right-skew chisels to carefully pare the bevels. Be sure your chisels are razor sharp, and make light cuts to avoid tearing the grain (as I've done here).

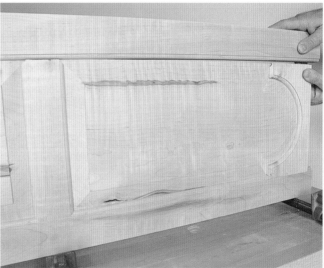

Assemble the tombstone door in the same manner as you would any other frame and panel door. Put everything together without glue to ensure that the parts actually do go together (and to admire your work!). Finish the panel, then glue up the assembly.

[CHAPTER *five*]

windows and glazed doors

Router bits for solid-panel work are scaled for cabinetry alone. In the realm of windows and glazed doors, however, bit manufacturers do have more than one scale of bit available. What may seem curious, though, is that the baseline bit set is scaled for window sashes, not cabinetry. Cabinetry sets are available, but they tend to be special-application cutters.

The explanation is that you can use most cope-and-stick sets to produce frames that will house glass rather than wood panels. The bit manufacturers don't document how you do it, but I will.

It turns out to be a great situation, because you do have a lot of options. With the bits now on the market, you can use your router table to make frames, showcases and display cases, glazed cabinet doors and even architectural windows and glazed passage doors.

All of the bits work in the same fundamental way — like cope-and-stick bits, in other words — but bit designers have incorporated some interesting wrinkles. Some bits actually help you produce frames with mortise-and-tenon joinery, for example. Other bits cut a bead you use to secure the glass at the same time that they cut the sticking profile.

Because of differences in scale, proportion

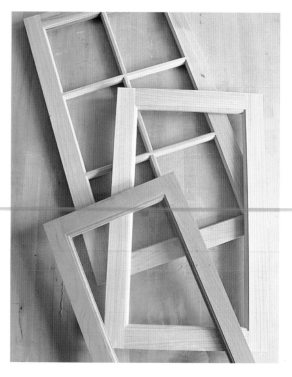

The same basic bits and techniques used to make frame and panel assemblies can be used to make glazed assemblies. Various specialized bits and bit sets broaden the spectrum from single-pane and divided-light cabinetry applications to include architectural doors and window sashes.

and stock thickness, none of the bits can produce both cabinetry and architectural frames. Pick a bit set that's appropriate for the project you have in mind. Don't expect one bit set to produce good results across the board.

USING CABINETRY COPE-AND-STICK BITS

To transform a cope-and-stick joint for a wooden panel into one that will accommodate a pane of glass, you need a rabbet instead of a groove. A simple alteration to the cope bit and an extra step, at the table saw, make this task easy to accomplish.

To supplant the groove-sized stub tenon with a rabbet-filling block, just remove the slotting cutter from the coping bit. You can do this with most two-bit sets and with bits that are reversible assemblies.

Loosen and remove the arbor nut from the bit, and pull off the slotting cutter. It's easy to do with the bit secured in the router collet so you can keep the bit from turning when you attack the arbor nut with your wrench. Use a sleeve-type spacer or a stack of washers to take up the vacated space on the arbor and replace the nut. Leave the bearing in place. That's all it takes.

Set the bit in your router table, adjust the height, position the fence and cope those rails. The cut will be nothing more than the negative of the profile.

The sticking cuts are made with the standard bit, no alterations needed. Set the bit and fence, then make the cuts. After these cuts are completed, go to the table saw and rip the back shoulder from the panel groove, transforming it into a rabbet. Be careful not to make the rabbet deeper than the groove; otherwise, you won't get a tight joint.

Assembly follows. To secure the glass, you can use glazing compound or slender wood strips that you glue in place or fasten with brads.

The upshot is that the same bits you use for frame and raised-panel cabinetry work can be your primary cutters for frame and glass-pane cabinetry work.

A cope-and-stick bit set designed for making frame and panel assemblies can usually be adapted to make assemblies with glass instead of wood panels. If you are making a set of built-in cabinets, for example, you can include glass doors that match the raised-panel doors.

To adapt your cope-and-stick bit set, remove the slotting cutter from the coping bit. You may need to use small washers or a sleeve-type spacer to fill a gap between the bearing and the threads on the arbor. Amana provides a flush-trimmer bit with its cope-and-stick sets for just this purpose.

Machine the rails and stiles with the sticking bit unaltered. Then rip each piece on the table saw to open the panel groove, transforming it into a rabbet. Set the blade high enough to remove the waste but without scoring the remaining shoulder. The fence position is critical. Align the cut with the bottom of the panel groove. If you cut any deeper, the ends of the rails won't seat tightly against the rabbet's shoulder.

Cope the rail ends first, just as you would in making a wood-panel door with this joinery. Set the fence tangent to the bit's bearing. Use a square-ended block to push the workpiece through the cut and to back up the good stock so exit blowout doesn't damage the frame part.

The mated pieces fit together nicely. The sticking profile nestles into the cope, and the butt of the rail seats tightly against the shoulder of the rabbet. The glue surface is mostly end grain to long grain, but where the base of the cope abuts the underside of the sticking profile there is a patch where long grain meets long grain.

USING SASH BITS

Suppose you want to make a window sash or a French door. The process is the same as the cabinetry process I've just described. What is different is the set of bits you use; it's all in the scale. Sash bits are designed to handle stock between 1" and 1½" thick, and the profile proportions are right for that stock thickness. One bit copes the rails, and the other cuts the sticking (and the sticking yields a rabbet, not a groove).

A lower-cost alternative to the conventional pair of bits is the reversible assembly. The profile cutter is an integral part of the shank and is topped by an arbor and pilot-bearing guide. The rabbet cutter can be removed from the arbor and replaced with a steel spacer. With this configuration, you raise the bit and cut the copes with the work's good face up. Put the rabbet cutter on the arbor, lower the bit and cut the sticking with the work's good face down.

Sash-cutter sets resemble cope-and-stick bits on steroids. That's because they are scaled to machine thicker stock than you'd use for cabinetry. The light blue bits are a matched pair: the cope cutter and the sticking bit. In a production setup, you'd be able to set up two router tables with them. The dark blue bit is a one-piece assembly. With both cutters on the arbor, it is a sticking bit. Convert it to a cope cutter by replacing the slotting cutter with a sleeve-type spacer.

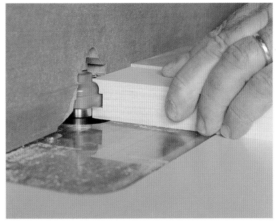

Coping is coping, whether you are machining a cabinet rail or a sash rail. Though it resembles a conventional edge-forming profile bit, this cope cutter has the pilot-bearing guide under the head so it references the butt of the rail rather than the shoulder of the profile cope.

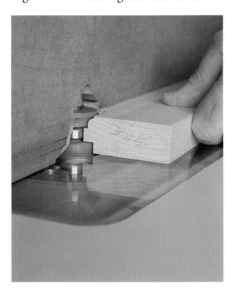

Sticking is sticking, too. The setup and sticking routine used with the sash set mimics that of a cabinetry set. Two factors distinguish this bit as a sash bit. Most obvious: It forms a rabbet rather than a groove. The proportion of the profile is different. It is deeper in relation to its width to compensate both for a difference in stock thickness — sashes are thicker than cabinet doors — and in "panel" thickness — glass panes are thinner than wood panels.

Here's the payoff: joining the rail and stile. The parts don't connect quite as well as those for a conventional cope-and-stick joint, but a frame assembled without glue holds together surprisingly well. When a sash is glued up, glazed, finished and cased, you need not worry about it falling apart.

DIVIDING THE FRAME

If you want to divide the framed area, you can make the divider strips with the same bits, whether modified cope-and-stick cutters for cabinetry or sash bits for architectural work. Though they are often (and interchangeably) called sash bars, the vertical divider is a mullion; the horizontal divider, a muntin. If you halve the opening, the divider obviously will be full-length or -width. If you divide the space for four or more panes, either the mullion or the muntin will need to be broken. The structure will be stronger if you segment the longer piece, but you can break up either one.

Because these parts are usually quite slender, you should adjust your proce-dures. Do as much work as you can with wide stock. Before you stick a sash bar that's been reduced to its final width, make yourself a custom pusher, as shown on page 120. The push block keeps your hands clear of the bit.

If you need two muntins and three mullions, for example, crosscut one wide blank for the muntins and one for the mullions. Cope the ends of these pieces and stick both long edges. Rip one mullion from the blank, then stick the remaining blank's "new" edge. Rip the second and third mullions from that blank and the muntins from the muntin blank. Then use the push block to hold the slender parts as you stick the second edge of each piece.

To assemble the divided frame, apply glue to the coped muntin and mullion ends as well as to the rail ends. Press the coped ends into the sticking on the stiles and rails and mullions and muntins.

Even a simple frame can be vexing to glue up. Add mullions and muntins and you have many more parts to hold in alignment. Having a panel to keep the parts in basic alignment is a big help. Trying to assemble the frame around glass panes is hazardous, so make tem-porary "panes" out of hardboard. Nip the corners off these "panes" so they don't get glued to the frame.

Clamp the assembly until the glue sets. Apply a finish, install the glass and the unit is completed.

Multipaned windows and doors can be constructed with sash bits and adapted cabinetry cope-and-stick bits by using them to produce narrow sash bars that partition the frame opening. Because the sash pro-file is scaled for this application, the sash bars look right, but sash bars made with the cabinetry bits look too wide.

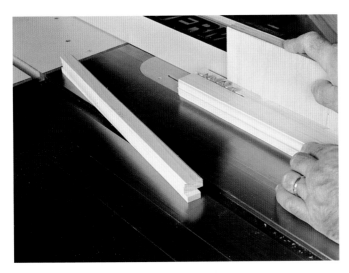

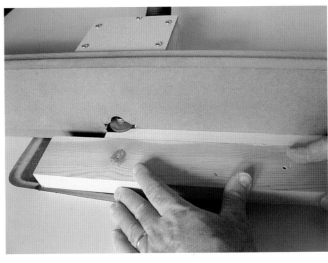

Sticking very narrow strips for muntins and mullions can be hazardous. As the profile is formed, it reduces the footprint of the strip on the tabletop and against the fence. The strip wants to tip or roll; it's just hard to manage safely. So do this: Crosscut and cope the ends of a piece about 3" to 4" wide. Rout the sticking profile on both edges, then rip strips of the desired width from the wider piece. The strips are ready for the next step in their manufacture.

To stick the parallel edge of the sash bar, tuck it into the push block (see "Sash Bar Push Block" on the next page). The push block holds the strip in proper alignment throughout the cut, and it keeps your fingers away from the cutting zone.

Assembling a sash frame is easy. Aligning the sash bars and keeping them square is what's vexing. Assembly "panes," pieces of plywood or hardboard cut to the dimensions of the glass panes, are a boon here. As you piece together the frame, set the panes in place. They keep the narrow sash bars in alignment, even as you apply clamps.

Sash Bar Push Block

To make a push block for sticking the sash bars, simply cope the long edge of a scrap of the working stock. It should be as long as the longest sash bar and about 3" wide. Screw a short strip of $\frac{1}{4}$"-thick material to one end. The tip of it should project about $\frac{3}{8}$" past the coped edge so it can catch the end of the sash bar. You can add a short piece of dowel to the push block if you want a handle.

To use the push block, tuck the stick edge of the sash bar into the cope, then feed the whole works along the router table fence to stick the sash bar's second edge.

Don't hesitate to view the push block as expendable. After sticking those long sash bars, cut the push block down to the length of the shorter sash bars.

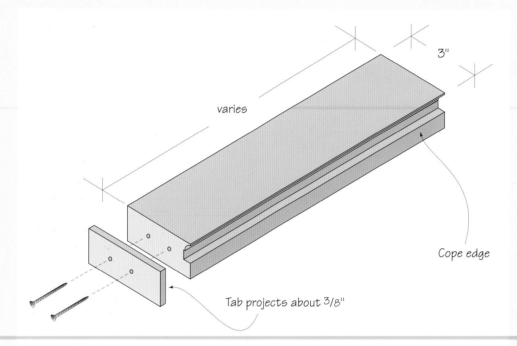

3"

varies

Cope edge

Tab projects about 3/8"

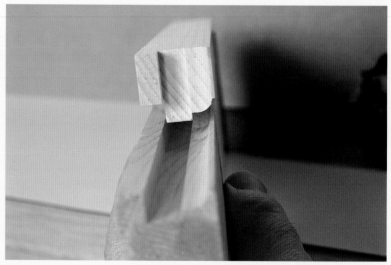

When it comes to routing the sticking on the narrow muntins and mullions, the cope-and-stick profile is your friend. The cope profile routed into the edge of your push block will hold a sticked piece surprisingly firmly. The heel screwed to the end of the push block prevents the sash bar from sliding out of the push block.

REINFORCING THE JOINTS

The hitch — there's always a hitch, isn't there?— here is the strength and longevity of the joinery. In a door, and especially in an architectural door, the joints need greater strength than a simple glued butt can provide. Yes, there is a little mechanical interlock, but the glue holds the parts together and the joint's gluing surface is almost nothing but end grain to long grain. Glass is heavy, and a door with six or more panes needs to be assembled with strong, enduring joinery.

One solution is to reinforce the joints with dowels or mortises and loose tenons. In some circumstances, dowels can be added to a joint after it has been glued and assembled: Drill through the edge of the stile into the joint, then drive a dowel into the hole.

Introducing mortises and loose tenons is manageable if you have a plunge router, an edge guide and a suitable work holder. Turn back to chapter two and read again about incorporating loose tenons into cope-and-stick joinery. Before making the window frame, rout mortises in both the rails and stiles. Plane down scraps of the working stock to make loose tenons. You can reinforce the sash-bar joinery with dowels. Use your router mortising setup to bore holes for the dowels. Having these joints not only strengthens the frame but makes it easier to assemble.

Specialty Bits

To make reinforced joinery for sashes and glazed cabinetry frames just a little easier to produce, a number of manufacturers make bits specifically designed to accommodate traditional mortise-and-tenon joinery.

An added benefit of these bits is that the profile is proportioned to the application. It is narrower than the sticking profile on standard cabinetry cope-and-stick cutters, and it is placed somewhat deeper on the stock. Thus

muntins and mullions cut using the bits are narrow, and the assembled frame looks right.

Several companies sell sash bit sets that have an inverted-head coping bit paired with a conventional sticking bit. These are scaled for thicker stock (usually between $1^{3}/_{16}$" and $1^{1}/_{2}$" thick). The design allows you to construct a window frame with the strength of traditional mortise-and-tenon joinery and the ease of assembly of coped sticking rather than mitered sticking.

Lay out and cut mortises and tenons for the rails and stiles, and even for sash bars. Then cope the ends of the rails and sash bars. The inverted-

Loose tenons are the perfect reinforcements for the joints in a sash or glazed door. You can rout mortises in the stiles and the ends of the rails either before or after the parts are profiled. In addition to strengthening the joinery, the loose tenons align the parts during assembly.

Inverted-head coping bits are designed specifically for coping rails that have integral tenons. The bit has no pilot-bearing. The cut must be guided by a low-profile fence, against which the shoulder of the coped profile rides. The tenon passes right over the cutter.

head bit design allows the tenon to pass over the cutter. Bear in mind that the coping bit doesn't have a pilot-bearing guide. A precisely positioned low-profile fence is essential for a joint that fits correctly.

With all that done, stick all the parts and assemble the frame.

Divided-Light Bits

The so-called divided-light bit set originated by Freud consists of a cope cutter and a sticking cutter.

The cope bit produces stub tenons at the same time that it forms the cope. This bit is just like a cabinetry cope cutter, but the sticking cutter doesn't cut a groove to accommodate the stub tenons. You have to cut mortises for them. In addition, you must trim the tenons, because they extend the width of the cope cut.

Cut these shallow mortises either before or after routing the copes and the sticking. Use whatever means you favor. Because the tenons are square cornered, the mortises also should be square cornered. You'll need to trim the width of the tenons on the rails so they aren't exposed on the ends of the assembly. Because of the configuration of the cope cut, you have to do this with hand tools.

Perhaps the biggest challenge is to lay out the locations of the mortises on the stiles, rails and sash bars. If you misalign matching mortises on the stiles, for example, the rails or sash bars will be cocked, and obviously so.

The divided-light bit set simplifies cutting the profile and rabbets for cabinetry frames on rails, stiles, muntins and mullions. The cut configurations force you into mortise-and-tenon joinery that makes the frame stronger. Without cutting mortises for the stub tenons formed in the cope cut, you can't join the cope and the stick.

One swell result of mortise-and-tenon joinery in a divided-light frame is that the many parts align positively during assembly. Spread out the parts and begin assembling them in the middle. Capture the inside mullion between the muntins, then fit those muntins to one stile. Add another mullion and a rail at the top, then add a mullion and rail at the bottom. The second stile is joined to the assembly last. None of the skinny bars slide out of position as you work, and their tenons are seated in mortises. After the glue has set and the clamps are off, those joints enhance the strength of the assembly.

The expeditious approach is to rout the copes and the sticking on all the parts. The stub tenons formed by the cope cut extend from edge to edge, and the sticking cut doesn't shorten them. On the rails, trim them back with a chisel (left). Leave full-width stub tenons on the mullions and muntins. Use the tenons to lay out the mortises on the flat between the profile and the rabbet. Then cut the mortises with a hollow chisel mortiser (far left). The tenons are stubby, so cut the mortises only $3/8$" to $1/2$" deep.

The Lonnie Bird Set

A different style of bits for divided-light cabinet doors was designed by furniture maker Lonnie Bird. If you use this three-bit set, you lay out and cut the mortises and tenons first. An inverted-head cutter produces the copes. The sticking is produced in two passes, one to cut the bead profile, the other to cut the glass rabbet. The big advantage with this system is that you can make tenons longer than $^3/_{16}$".

The process begins with an assembly drawing that shows the design and dimensions of the door. Many cabinet-makers advocate doing a full-size drawing so you can lay the actual parts on the drawing to transfer key layout points.

Begin the layout process with a stile, marking the mortise locations for the top and bottom rails, then for each muntin. Clamp the second stile and any mullions edge to edge, and transfer the layout marks from the master stile. Next, lay out the tenons on the muntins, mullions and rails.

After cutting the mortises and tenons, by whatever means you prefer, do the copes. Adjust the cope bit's height by raising it until it just skims the tenon. Then make and position the fence. Because the typical fence will interfere with the tenon, use a strip of $^1/_4$"-thick plywood instead. Make a cutout in the center for the bit. The tenon shoulder can ride along this low fence, and a block can serve as both a push block and blowout prevention. Position the fence carefully and clamp it to the tabletop, then cope the rails and the muntin and mullion blanks.

With this set, the complex sticking cut — meaning both the profile and the glass rabbet, usually made in a single pass — takes two operations to complete. The first forms the profile with a quarter-round beading bit (a bit that looks commonplace but that is matched to the cope cutter). The rabbet is cut separately with a rabbeting bit.

Use the "rout then rip then rout again" routine to profile the muntins and mullions. Use a sash bar push block to do the slender pieces. For the rabbet cuts, make a second push block to hold the muntins and mullions steady.

After shaping all the pieces, clamp up the assembly without glue to check how everything fits. Then proceed to final glue-up.

Lonnie Bird's CMT divided-light door set allows you to incorporate longer tenons in the joinery, thanks to the inverted-head cope cutter. The set includes separate beading and rabbeting bits to cut the sticking, though it isn't clear what advantage there is to that. The number of operations is increased, and the setups become more finicky.

The inverted-head configuration of the coping bit allows it to cut the cope without inference from the tenon, which passes just above it. Obviously, you have to cut the tenon first. Use a $^1/_4$"-thick fence to guide this cut.

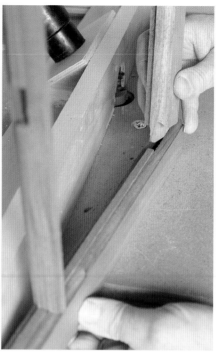

Rout the rabbets for the glass in the parts. This cut removes the final obstacle to assembling the joints.

After cutting and fitting the mortises and tenons and coping the rails, mullions and muntins, rout the sticking profile with the beading bit. The profile should just break the shoulder of the mortises.

SECURING THE GLASS

Assemble the sash or door parts cut with any of these sets, and you'll have a sturdy, attractive unit ready for glazing. What you won't have is an integrated means of securing the glass. You must use glazing points and compound or make retainer strips.

Recoverable Bead

A recoverable bead bit set features a standard cope cutter. The sticking bit is special, though, because it cuts a profile on both edges and leaves a slot between them. One moulded edge projects $1/8$" beyond the other. This is the width of a table saw blade's kerf, so you can rip that molded strip from the part, then use it to secure the glass. It will be the same size as the sticked bead.

The sticking bit is big ($2^3/8$" diameter and 3" high), so it must be used in a router table and run at a reduced speed (16,000 rpm maximum). In setting up the bit, you must set the bit height to center the slot on the stock's edge. Because the bit has no pilot-bearing guide, the fence must guide the work and control the width of the cut. Setting the fence is a little tricky. Sight

Installing glass in a window sash typically involves the use of glazing points and glazing compound. Prime the sash before installing the glass. Spread glazing compound in the rabbet, press the glass into the compound and drive glazing points into the rabbet to secure the glass. Then use a putty knife to apply and groom the glazing compound to cover the glazing points and to shed water.

A glazed frame or door ought to be treated differently than a window sash. You can use hardwood strips, perhaps profiled, to secure the glass panes. The strips can be glued in place or fastened with brads.

along it across the cutting edges to get a starting position. Then begin a test-cut, running it 8" to 12". Stop and look at the sample to make sure you are getting the full profile. Set the sample back on

the bit (with the router not running), and, if necessary, shift the fence so it is against the test strip on both infeed and outfeed sides of the bit.

If you want to make the cut in

stages, first set the fence for the final cut. Then clamp stop blocks against the back edge of the fence on either side; these will capture the final fence position. You can now shift the fence forward to reduce the bite. Before making the final pass, push the fence back against the stop blocks.

When ripping the recoverable bead free of the work, set the table saw's fence carefully. If you skim material off the shoulder of the rabbet, the butts of the rails won't seat against it. The joint will have a gap, which will weaken the joint.

After the cabinet door frame is assembled, securing the glass is a matter of fitting the bead strips, mitering their ends and gluing them in place. The completed door looks very finished from either side.

Freud's recoverable bead bit set for making glazed frames and doors can save you some time and materials and enable you to produce glazed cabinet assemblies that sport a finished appearance both inside and out. The sticking bit profiles both edges. You rip one of the profiles from the rails and stiles and save the offcut to secure the glass.

Here are samples of the sticking before (right) and after (left) the recoverable bead is ripped off using the table saw. Straight off the bit, one bead is proud of the other by $\frac{1}{8}$". Rip the proud bead free of the frame part.

Fit the recovered bead strips into the back of the frame to hold the glass in place. As you trim the strips to fit, miter the ends. Glue them in place.

Flexible Rubber Retainer

A rubber retainer strip is a different solution to the glazing method. A bit set designed by Marc Sommerfeld adds a special slotting cutter to a conventional sash set. You rout the rails and stiles in the usual way, then you use the special slotting cutter to slot the shoulder of the rabbet. After you assemble the door and place the glass, you press into the slot a flexible plastic retainer, which secures the glass.

To cut the slot in just the right location, lay the workpiece facedown on the router table. Adjust the bit so its shank-mounted bearing rides on the delicate edge of the sticked profile. That will give you the correct slot depth, and it should position the retainer to hold the glass without it rattling.

The rails can be slotted from end to end, but you should stop the slots before you get to the ends of the stiles. Otherwise, they'll show on the top and bottom of the assembled door.

Marc Sommerfeld, a master of quick and easy, has designed a whole passel of gadgets to simplify common woodworking operations. This set of three bits, made by CMT, is another of Sommerfeld's innovations. Two of the bits are straightforward: One cuts the cope and the other cuts the sticking for ogee-profiled glazed frames and doors. It's the third bit that's clever. This special slotting cutter has a special bearing and is used to slot the inner edges of the rails and stiles to house a flexible plastic retainer for the glass.

After coping the rails then sticking both the rails and stiles, rout a narrow slot for the rubber strip that holds the glass in the assembled frame. The slotting cutter is unique to this set and has a very narrow bearing on the shank. When the bearing is aligned with the edge of the ogee sticking profile, the slot will be properly aligned (top). Rout the slot in the rails from end to end. In the stiles, make a stopped slot. Mark the center of the bit on the fence; on the stile, mark the point where the edge of the rail will abut. Line up the two marks and begin the slot there (bottom).

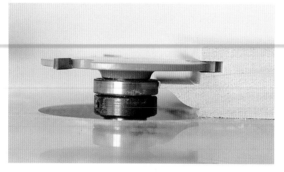

After the frame is assembled and the glass is cut to size, drop the glass into the rabbet and insert the rubber retainer in the slot. The retainer strip stays in place without glue and can easily be pulled out if the glass must be replaced. Use a utility knife to miter the retainer strips at the corners.

suppliers

AMANA TOOL
120 Carolyn Boulevard
Farmingdale, NY 11735
800-445-0077
www.amanatool.com
High-quality saw blades, router bits and shaper cutters. Sells through dealers.

BENCH DOG
3310 Fifth Street NE
Minneapolis, MN 55418
800-786-8902
www.benchdog.com
Router tables, router lifts and associated products

BUSY BEE TOOLS
355 Norfinch Drive
North York, ON M3N 1Y7
800-461-2879
www.busybeetools.com
Retailer of tools, accessories and supplies.

FREUD TOOLS
218 Feld Avenue
High Point, NC 27263
800-334-4107
www.freudtools.com
High-quality saw blades, router bits and shaper cutters. Sells through dealers.

HIGHLAND HARDWARE
1045 N. Highland Avenue NE
Atlanta, GA 30306
800-241-6748
www.highlandhardware.com
Retailer of tools, accessories and supplies.

INFINITY CUTTING TOOLS
2762 Summerdale Drive
Clearwater, FL 33761
877-872-2487
www.infinitytools.com
High-quality saw blades, router bits and shaper cutters. Sells direct.

LEE VALLEY
U.S.:
P.O. Box 1780
Ogdensburg, NY 13669-6780
800-267-8735
Canada:
P.O. Box 6295, Station J
Ottawa, ON K2A 1T4
800-267-8761
www.leevalley.com
Woodworking tool manufacturer (Veritas) and supercatalog retailer of tools, accessories, supplies and hardware.

MICROFENCE
13160 Saticoy Street
North Hollywood, CA 91605
818-982-4367
www.microfence.com
Finest router edge guide (and kindred accessories) known to woodworking.

PAT WARNER
1427 Kenora Street
Escondido, CA 92027-3940
760-747-2623
www.patwarner.com
High-quality router accessories, jigs and fixtures, and sound router woodworking information.

REID TOOL SUPPLY
2265 Black Creek Road
Muskegon, MI 49441
800-253-0421
www.reidtool.com
Extensive catalog of machinist's tools, hardware and fascinating widgets. First place to look for toggle clamps, plastic knobs and other jigmaking hardware.

ROCKLER WOODWORKING AND HARDWARE
4365 Willow Drive
Medina, MN 55340
800-279-4441
www.rockler.com
Supercatalog retailer of tools, accessories, supplies and hardware.

WOODCENTRAL
www.woodcentral.com
Woodworking forum — discussion boards, project gallery, book and tool reviews, article archive and lots more.

WOODHAVEN
501 W. First Avenue
Durant, IA 52747-9729
800-344-6657
www.woodhaven.com
Router tables, woodworking jigs and fixtures, router bits and more.

WOODLINE USA
www.woodline.com
Extensive catalog of affordable router bits and shaper cutters. Sells direct.

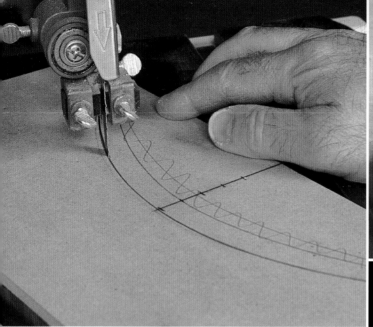
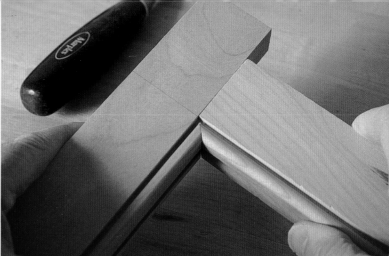

index